Through skilful and penetrating prose [...]
of Samson that is as far removed from [...]
chalk is from cheese. Vivid, stark, cha [...] s
illuminating – the stereotype of Samson is stripped away to reveal [...] *le*
power he wielded and the influences to which he succumbed.
John Glass, General Superintendent, Elim

I have always loved Jeff Lucas's balanced, realistic and honest approach to
Christianity and humanity. This book is no exception! The reader will be
challenged, encouraged, energised and strengthened into facing the future
with a different approach, rather than a resigned acceptance of imperfection.
It is a topic to which all of us can relate in some measure. Jeff's honest,
sometimes blunt 21st-century interpretation of the life story of Samson is
riveting and should challenge everyone – and mostly we'll understand, but
not necessarily like, what we read!
Fiona Castle OBE, writer and speaker

'I like Jeff Lucas and I like this book because it has reminded me that
God's grace is bigger than my many failures and His strength is somehow
made perfect in weakness. Jeff has made the story of Samson relevant and
inspirational for a new generation.'
Pete Greig, Alpha International and 24-7 Prayer

Riveting stuff! Living faithfully in our highly sexualised culture is one of the
biggest challenges for Christian discipleship. Jeff Lucas applies his unique 'tell
it as it is' to the familiar story of Samson and his unexpurgated interpretation
is a compelling read. It will inspire you to believe that Jesus really does work
on rubbish heaps.
David Coffey OBE, Global Ambassador for BMS World Mission

With warmth, vulnerability and keen biblical insight, Jeff brings hope through
a familiar story that shines with significance through his writing. Highly
recommended.
R.T. Kendall, former Minister of Westminster Chapel, London

This powerful, prophetic, perceptive and provocative book should be a
bestseller. It reads like a Grisham novel – a real page-turner.
Lyndon Bowring, Executive Chairman of CARE

THERE ARE NO STRONG PEOPLE

THERE ARE NO STRONG PEOPLE

JEFF LUCAS

CWR

Dedication

To Stanley Benjamin and Alexander David.
May you grow to become men of God:
strengthened by the Spirit, blessed because of grace,
beautiful in character and faithful until the end.

With much love, Grandad.

Published 2012 by CWR, Waverley Abbey House,
Waverley Lane, Farnham, Surrey GU9 8EP, UK.
Registered Charity No. 294387.
Registered Limited Company No. 1990308.
Reprinted 2013

See back of book for list of National Distributors.

Unless otherwise indicated, all Scripture references are
from the Holy Bible: New International Version (NIV),
copyright © 1973, 1978, 1984 by Biblica, formerly the
International Bible Society.

P. 178: Excerpts from Lea Goldberg poem used with
permission of The Toby Press Ltd.

Concept development, editing, design and production
by CWR.

Cover image: istockphoto.com/vetta
Printed in Finland by Bookwell
ISBN: 978-1-85345-624-4

Contents

Straining all his nerves, he bowed.

As with the force of winds and waters pent,

When mountains tremble,

those two massy pillars

With horrible convulsion to and fro

He tugged, he shook, till down

they came and drew

The whole roof after them,

with burst of thunder

Upon the heads of all who sat beneath,

Lords, ladies, captains, counsellors, or priests,

Their choice nobility and flower.

Samson Agonistes, Milton

Preface

I'll keep this short.

First, a word on how to get the best out of this book. While this is not a Bible study, I'd like to ask a favour. At the beginning of each of the four sections, there's a portion of biblical text. Please, *don't* do as I sometimes do and skip over the Scripture that's included there. In fact, why not go the extra mile and read the text twice over? And then maybe even put this book down and ponder the text for a while. It's good to let the story tell itself, before anything else is added. Let your imagination be fired by this ancient but compelling epic, the story of Samson. Better still, read the whole of Judges before you start. That way you'll get to see the big picture context to Samson's strange story.

And then, just a word about whom this book is for. Rather obviously, this is a book about a man, but it's not just for men – on the contrary. The battles of life might be approached differently by each of the genders, but they are basically the same skirmishes – to claim anything less is to meander into stereotypes. Samson's story has been recorded for the benefit of humanity, not just men's conferences.

That said, I won't avoid some of the more boisterous aspects of the story. Actually, boisterous is a sanitised way of saying 'lurid', or, even more accurately, 'raunchy'. Brace yourself. Samson is best known for his energetic coupling with the gorgeous but poisonous Delilah. But without sounding too much like Tom Jones, one of the questions that I'd like us to consider (I'd love to say answer, but that's too ambitious) is simply this:

Why, why, why, Delilah?

Also, as we trace this strange tale of a man called to the heights but who had a penchant for the low life, let's bear in mind that Samson's story is in fact three stories – that of Samson himself, of Israel and of the God of Israel. The three stories don't run in rigid parallel, but are woven together inextricably. So, as we'll see, Samson engages in some quick-on-the-draw choices that God never intended. In doing so, he shows himself to be a man of his times, reflecting Israel's moral and spiritual condition at that low-ebb time in her chequered history. But then God intersects with Samson's headstrong, hormonally driven antics and uses some of his independent bullishness to get His purposes fulfilled. Remember this idea of three interacting stories, as it will save you getting confused later on.

Samson's story is told at a breathless pace – which means that there will always be a variety of conclusions drawn from the account of his life. That's the intention of storytelling: to nudge the imagination and even fuel speculation. Sometimes totally different conclusions are reached. One of the most famous recent literary works on Samson is *Lion's Honey* by David Grossman. A contemporary writer and liberal Israeli political activist, Grossman regards Samson critically but sympathetically, painting him (with stunning prose) as a tormented individual who opts to end his life in order to end his suffering. Another, more classic work is *Samson* by Ze'ev Jabotinsky, a twentieth-century author and nationalistic Jewish political activist, who regarded Samson as a heroic figure exemplifying the ultimate Jewish freedom fighter, who killed himself to help his people. I've considered the reflections of dozens of commentators and have found that Samson is an enigmatic figure who still polarises opinion.

Commentators wildly disagree about him. And that's all right. Let's mull over his life together and consider the implications of his journey without the pressure of trying to be absolutely right or final in any conclusions we might reach.

Also, bear in mind that Samson was not a Christian trapped in an Old Testament era, so let's not demand more of him than we should. (This often happens when Christians get hold of Samson, or any other Old Testament character, for that matter.) Yes, he slaughters many and he doesn't know any better, as no one told him to love his enemies. Alexander Maclaren says it well: 'Instead of trying to make a lofty hero out of Samson, it is far better to recognise frankly the limitations of his character and the imperfections of his religion.'[1]

What is certain is that the story of Samson (and especially his dalliance with Delilah) is very much a part of public consciousness. The makers of Weetabix used a parody of the seduction/haircutting scene to advertise their product. In their version, Samson got the girl and the haircut, but, fortunately for him, had Weetabix for breakfast that day and so managed to beat off the attack of the Philistines.[2] This is a well-known drama of love, revenge, lust, betrayal – and faith. But familiarity can breed contempt – and preconceptions. Let's try to put any prejudice to one side and approach this odd man's life with open hearts and minds.

And no, of course he didn't eat Weetabix.

One more detail: there's been a fair amount of discussion among scholars about whether or not the Samson story actually happened, or if it's a saga or myth. Recent scholarship tends towards accepting it as a historical fact, with the understanding that Jewish storytelling veers towards hyperbole. And, as one scholar (who doesn't believe that it is historical narrative) said, 'Whether it is historical fact or not, we're meant to treat it as if it is'.[3]

So I will. Hey, ancient rabbis did. The writer to the Hebrews did. So I'm in good company ...

So welcome, ladies and gentlemen. Brace yourselves, please. Here we go ...

Jeff Lucas

Colorado 2011

Book One
BEGINNINGS

Again the Israelites did evil in the eyes of the LORD, so the LORD delivered them into the hands of the Philistines for forty years.

A certain man of Zorah, named Manoah, from the clan of the Danites, had a wife who was sterile and remained childless. The angel of the LORD appeared to her and said, 'You are sterile and childless, but you are going to become pregnant and give birth to a son. Now see to it that you drink no wine or other fermented drink and that you do not eat anything unclean, because you will conceive and give birth to a son. No razor may be used on his head because the boy is to be a Nazirite, set apart to God from birth, and he will begin the deliverance of Israel from the hands of the Philistines.'

Then the woman went to her husband and told him, 'A man of God came to me. He looked like an angel of God, very awesome. I didn't ask him where he came from, and he didn't tell me his name. But he said to me, "You will conceive and give birth to a son. Now then, drink no wine or other fermented drink and do not eat anything unclean, because the boy will be a Nazirite of God from birth until the day of his death."'

Then Manoah prayed to the LORD: 'O Lord, I beg you, let the man of God you sent to us come again to teach us how to bring up the boy who is to be born.'

God heard Manoah, and the angel of God came again to the woman while she was out in the field; but her husband Manoah was not with her. The woman hurried to tell her husband, 'He's here! The man who appeared to me the other day!'

Manoah got up and followed his wife. When he came to the man, he said, 'Are you the one who talked to my wife?'

'I am,' he said.

So Manoah asked him, 'When your words are fulfilled, what is to be the rule for the boy's life and work?'

The angel of the LORD answered, 'Your wife must do all that I have told her. She must not eat anything that comes from the grapevine, nor drink any wine or other fermented drink nor eat anything unclean. She must do everything I have commanded her.'

Manoah said to the angel of the LORD, 'We would like you to stay until we prepare a young goat for you.'

The angel of the LORD replied, 'Even though you detain me, I will not eat any of your food. But if you prepare a burnt offering, offer it to the LORD.' (Manoah did not realise that it was the angel of the LORD.)

Then Manoah enquired of the angel of the LORD, 'What is your name, so that we may honour you when your word comes true?'

He replied, 'Why do you ask my name? It is beyond understanding.'

Then Manoah took a young goat, together with the grain offering, and sacrificed it on a rock to the LORD. And the LORD did an amazing thing while Manoah and his wife watched:

As the flame blazed up from the altar toward heaven, the angel of the LORD ascended in the flame. Seeing this, Manoah and his wife fell with their faces to the ground.

When the angel of the LORD did not show himself again to Manoah and his wife, Manoah realised that it was the angel of the LORD.

'We are doomed to die!' he said to his wife. 'We have seen God!'

But his wife answered, 'If the LORD had meant to kill us, he would not have accepted a burnt offering and grain offering from our hands, nor shown us all these things or now told us this.'

The woman gave birth to a boy and named him Samson. He grew and the LORD blessed him, and the Spirit of the LORD began to stir him while he was in Mahaneh Dan, between Zorah and Eshtaol.[1]

One:
GOOD PEOPLE DO BAD THINGS

'Perhaps the rabbis knew what we often overlook ... there has never been a hero without flaws.' – Louis Ginzberg[1]

It wasn't Mrs Jennings' fault that I became a heretic.

Mrs Jennings.

I bring her name to mind now and am instantly transported back in time, squirming on a small wooden chair in Sunday school, half a century ago. There is a semicircle of fidgety five-year-olds, neatly arranged around Mrs Jennings; our chairs scrape on the knots of the scrubbed pine floorboards of the Baptist Church 'fellowship hall'. There is insipid orange squash, diluted into uselessness, being passed around in flimsy plastic cups halfway through the lesson. A chocolate biscuit follows – a priceless delicacy in the eyes of a five-year-old.

Pinned to the walls by oversized brass drawing pins is the scrawled crayon artwork of the younger kids, fluorescent yellow and blue and green, their names in the corners larger than the stick figures they've created.

My heresy (not so much a heresy really, more a ridiculous idea) was twofold.

It was that Moses once jumped out of an aircraft and that bad children would be punished by having their brains slowly boiled.

To the latter first, lest I imply that Mrs Jennings was a threatening bully. She was 200 years old, or so it seemed to me at the time, and she was a Sunday school teacher in the swinging sixties so was permanently disgusted. But she was not a monster.

The Baptists used overhead gas heaters in a vain attempt to warm their frigid building. Hanging down from the ceiling, a dangling chain to switch them on and off, they would crackle and hiss and sometimes even spit. If you were seated right under one of them, the top of your head would soon heat up, sending you to sleep. Worse, I feared, they might cause your brains to bubble in your skull. The idea that they could be used to punish wayward children probably drifted into my heated head one drowsy Sunday morning.

But back to Mrs Jennings.

She *was* responsible for my belief that Moses was a skydiver.

It was the flannelgraph she used.

Perhaps you're not familiar with flannelgraph.

How about fuzzy-felt? Same thing.

Flannelgraph was beloved by Sunday school teachers five decades ago. A khaki flannel cloth was stretched out over an easel. The long-suffering teacher would press sticky-backed characters onto the board while telling a Bible story. This was primitive multimedia, PowerPoint before Bill Gates.

There was David the shepherd boy, all freckles and flyaway hair, armed with his trusty sling. Goliath, like Brutus out of *Popeye*, muscles like pistons, stubbly bun of a chin, huge gritted teeth.

Jesus, bizarrely blonde for a Jew, white flowing gown, wan half-smile, always hotly pursued by fat, fluffy sheep.

And Moses the skydiver. At least that's what I thought he was, because he invariably toppled headfirst from the flannel board before the story ended. Fifty years of theological reflection later, I know that skydiving wasn't part of the biblical narrative. Moses just needed a stickier back.

The flannelgraph was supposed to bring the stories and characters of Scripture to life. But it didn't work for me. I'd peer into David's boyish face and couldn't find a hint of fear in those eyes, even though he stood tiny in Goliath's long shadow. Jesus looked ever ready to bless in an otherworldly way and seemed to have no problem with walking around while permanently looking up at the sky. Those figures gave no hint of out-loud laughter. They didn't sweat, rage or doubt. Inexpertly cut from a teachers' manual, their only imperfections came from clumsy scissor work that created jagged edges.

But the leading women and men of the Bible are not unwaveringly consistent, nor clean cut either, for the most part. In telling us their stories, Scripture portrays most of them as highly effective people with some questionable habits. No airbrushing treatment for them, they are shown as they were, deep flaws included. They were cut from flesh, not paper. Turning to the pages of Scripture, I remember the strict instructions Oliver Cromwell gave to his portrait painter: 'Remark all these roughnesses, pimples, warts and everything as you see me, otherwise I will never pay a farthing for it.'[2]

I've seen some of those canvases and Oliver was no pretty boy. In one, he sports a wart so big, it threatens to take over his face.

Scripture paints its heroes with similar honesty.

There's Noah, famous for faithful boat-building, who exposed himself in a drunken sprawl. His son, Ham, peeks into his father's tent and, at best, some nudge-nudge-wink-wink finger pointing follows. At worst, there's a hint of incestuous sex. Not exactly the way for humanity's new first family to behave. But the message is clear. Even after the flood, when humans are around, things are messy.

And the warts-and-all chronicles continue, as fugitive Jonah preaches the most effective (and brief) sermonette in history, then stomps off in an outraged sulk when an entire city repents. He loathes those wicked people of Nineveh and then whines at God about his lack of a sunshade.

Father of faith Abraham and his geriatric wife Sarah hear of impossible blessing – they are as good as dead, but are suddenly told they will be expecting – and then laugh in the face of the blesser. Sarah suggests a quick fix to their childlessness and leads her husband to her servant's bed.

Elijah, skilled at summoning fire from heaven and good at stirring corpses to life, runs for his life and then prays for death.

Peter swears and denies knowing his best friend. Three times.

From the Garden at the beginning to the City at the end, Scripture tells the story of God getting His will done through some very dubious characters.

And perhaps Samson is the most dubious of them all.

Jewish children are taught to call him 'Samson the hero'. Elite Israeli combat units have been named in his honour and Israel's nuclear programme was called 'The Samson Option'.[3] But he's the Bible's most famous bad boy; history generally remembers his sins more than his exploits. His story is not for the faint-hearted.

After all, some view him as a suicide bomber.

His grand finale did not involve an actual bomb – they hadn't been invented yet. But Samson took out the Philistine temple, deliberately killing himself and many of his enemies, so some say the bomber parallel might be justified. We'll see.

His story is a saga of stomach-turning violence, merciless vengeance and high-stakes gambling.

And there's plenty of graphic sex, too.

Throughout history, Christian commentators and writers have called Samson plenty of names.[4]

Profligate judge.

The embodiment of all that was wrong with Israel.

The bawdy giant.

An obstreperous lout.

The oversexed muscleman.

A reckless, irresponsible practical joker.

A man full of high spirits and low ethics.

The noble savage.

Trickster.

Bandit.

A judge who chased women instead of enemies and who only avenged personal grievances.

An anti-hero.

Judge and fool.

A dead end.

A tragic figure, forever blind to the larger purposes of his God.

A selfish, shallow-minded playboy who squandered his talents.

Such sweeping statements are usually unjust and I'm uncomfortable with these generalisations.

It's not that I want to gloss over Samson's glaring faults, as some have tried to do. Samson was a man with serious issues. We don't need to try to rehabilitate him by minimalising his failures, or trying to explain them away. It's even been suggested that Samson consorted with prostitutes as part of an elaborate military strategy in a holy war, just as Joshua's spies went to the house of Rahab the harlot.[5]

But that's a big stretch. Joshua's spies sought *refuge* in a prostitute's house. Samson's visit was about sex, not military intelligence. We're told that Samson 'went in' to the prostitute – the graphic euphemism is intentional.

And then one ancient Jewish telling[6] of the Samson story edits out his visit to the prostitute totally, insisting instead that he just went to stay at an inn. Some in the fourth-century Church tried to tag Samson as a saint; others objected and sought to smear him as a figure of the antichrist. The man who apparently loved to fight has prompted many more skirmishes over the years.

Surely Samson knew how to be bad. But then, don't we all?

Consider humanity. There are some who are stunningly evil, who deserve the description 'monster'. They abuse and maim without compunction, gouging their way through life. Some even delight in the carnage, relishing every moment, hungry for more. They are very bad.

Jack the Ripper, who crept through the billowing Whitechapel fog, surgical bag in hand.

Fred West, who raped, tortured and murdered at least eleven women (including one of his own children), and then ended his own pain by knotting a hangman's noose in his cell. Was this his last act of domination and control?

But then, there are the epically good souls. Great in their silent selflessness, they pour out their lives for others. With the greatest respect to Mother Teresa, don't allow her image into your mind for a moment. There are countless others who have never stepped near the foul pavements of Calcutta and have never been celebrated for their goodness but, in the shadows, their kindness continues, even more remarkable because it is unknown.

And then there are the rest of us, the vast majority.

Capable of good and bad, sacrifice and selfishness, we spend our days hovering between good and evil, neither monsters nor saints.

Samson was not a heartless psychopath and he certainly wasn't a saint. I think that he just wanted what we all want, but looked in the wrong place for it. And that's why his life has so much to teach us all.

In an address given at a pastors' seminar at Northwest Theological Seminary, Robert Starke reminded all there – and us too – that we have much in common with the Bible's so-called bad boy:

> *Samson's story is our story as well. Again, not in some moralistic sense, that somehow we must avoid the ethical pitfalls that Samson could not. But, rather, we, like Samson, in union with Christ, stand between two pillars, between two ages. In Christ, we have been endued with the Spirit*

of God and yet struggle with the flesh. Like Samson, in Christ, we drink from the living water that flows from the Rock, all the while dwelling in Philistine territory. Spiritually blind, we have been made to see through faith. Like Samson, our strength is made perfect in weakness. Like Samson, we cry out in faith to Him who is able to deliver us. We too look in faith to the One who is able to save us completely. We embrace Jesus Christ by faith, just as Samson embraced those pillars. We participate in the glories of the age to come, even now. No longer shackled by the power of sin, death and hell, we, who were brought down, have been raised up in glory through the death and resurrection of our Judge – Jesus Christ. Like Samson, we cannot 'be like other men'. We are even now, being conformed to the image of Samson's Judge and our Judge. We have entered into the age to come. Together, we long for that final day when 'we will be like Him, because we will see Him, just as He is'.[7]

- - - - -

Perhaps Samson was not just a testosterone-charged buffoon, but yet another human being searching for home, for a place to lay his head.

He was a man of great faith and folly both. Sound familiar?

Picture him now.

He has plotted mayhem. Fuelled by fury at his enemies, he has spent the whole night scouring the undergrowth, trapping foxes. Three hundred of them. He has an improbable, insane scheme in mind. He spends many hours turning them into 150 squirming pairs, furiously unwilling partners, their tails braided together. They claw and writhe and snap their heads back and try to bite him, or each other. And now the really tricky part – he ties a torch to the joining of each of the two tails, the searing heat sending the squealing foxes into frantic terror.

And he releases them into the grain fields …

Watch them in their last terrible, chaotic journey. At first, the stronger of the pair gets its way, surges forward, dragging its partner helplessly along. But then it tires and the other digs in and so, for a few feet, the two head back in the other direction. This way and that, they zigzag across the tall heads of grain, their darting quickly igniting flames among the dry stalks. One hundred and fifty of them: soon the vineyards, groves and fields are a wall of fire. And the foxes end their agonising dance of death, their charred skeletons littering the scorched fields, the signatures of the artist of destruction …

Samson.

In a story so laden with imagery, perhaps the writer was here offering us an image of Samson himself. Standing between two pillars at the end of the story, there he is, a man impossibly pulled apart, drawn endlessly between good and evil. Called to be a carrier of light and a deliverer of judgment, he spends his days darting this way and that, a relentless tug of war within him.

Surely the image is of us, too. Let's not decide that we are so *good* that we are not capable of great evil. Those who exclaim with horror at the sins of others and insist, 'I could never do that', worry me deeply, because then we forget that we are all cousins to the Nazis. Given the right pressures and influence, we are capable of what seems unimaginable.

Yahiel Dinur, an Auschwitz concentration camp survivor, was called to testify against Adolf Eichmann at the Nuremberg trials in 1961. When Dinur saw his old oppressor in the courtroom, he fainted. He later said that his shock was caused by the realisation that the Eichmann who stood before him at the trial was not the god-like army officer who had sent millions to their death. This Eichmann, he said, was an ordinary man, an unremarkable man. And if this Eichmann was so ordinary, so human, said Dinur, then he realised that what Eichmann had done, any man could be capable of doing - even Yahiel Dinur. Dinur asserted, 'I saw that I am capable of doing this. I am as capable as him.'[8]

Evil can have a very ordinary face. Alexander Solzhenitsyn sums up our condition succinctly:

> One and the same human being is, at various ages, under various circumstances, a totally different human being. At times he is close to being a devil, at times to sainthood.[9]

You and I are capable of great evil - or great good.

There is a contradiction within us; an internal civil war that can and must be won.

Paul put it like this:

> I do not understand what I do. For what I want to do I do not do, but what I hate I do. And if I do what I do not want to do, I agree that the law is good. As it is, it is no longer I myself who do it, but it is sin living in me. I know that nothing good lives in me, that is, in my sinful nature. For I have the desire to do what is good, but I cannot carry it out. For what I do is not the good I want to do; no, the evil I do not want to do - this I keep on doing. Now if I do what I do not want to do, it is no longer I who do it,

but it is sin living in me that does it. So I find this law at work: When I want to do good, evil is right there with me.

For in my inner being I delight in God's law; but I see another law at work in the members of my body, waging war against the law of my mind and making me a prisoner of the law of sin at work within my members. What a wretched man I am! Who will rescue me from this body of death? Thanks be to God – through Jesus Christ our Lord![10]

It's true. Samson's story is for all of us. Like him, we are weak. But Samson's God is our God too.

TWO:
THERE ARE NO STRONG PEOPLE

'When the spirit of God came upon him he
could step with one stride from Zorah to
Eshtaol, while the hairs of his head arose
and clashed against one another so that they
could be heard for a like distance. He was
so strong that he could uplift two mountains
and rub them together like two clods of
earth.' – The Jewish Talmud, on Samson[1]

Strong.

It's a thick, solid word. It sounds tensile. A sumo word.
Strong squats in any sentence. Here are some examples:

The searing pain tormented her, jolting through her
nerves in cruel waves, but she stayed *strong* to the end.

His arms trembled under the impossible burden, but
at last, his face a shining mask of sweat and grimace,
the *strong* man thrust the weight-bar high ...

For a moment, she thought her heart would melt in terror
and then she remembered her father's words: 'Don't
let them smell fear. Be *strong*, girl. You can do this.'

Strong.

It's what we hope we'd be if we were tested. No one aspires to be timid, or wants to be fearful. On the contrary, weakness and addiction often come as a great surprise, stunning us with the knock-out punch reality that, yes, *we* could be so ensnared.

We pray that we'd be strong if, in the small hours of the night, a bedside telephone jangles and, in an instant, hauls us out of deep sleep. A policeman's voice, clipped and formal, launches us into a waking nightmare.

We'd want to be strong if a doctor, grim-faced, steps into the room to deliver the ominous test results.

We wonder how we'd do if we were summoned to war. Would we cope with the bloody butchery of a battlefield? We hope that we'd be strong and not run away from the carnage screaming, insane with terror.

No one has ambitions to be a coward. We want to be strong.

Strength.

Aside from epic naughtiness, it's what Samson is most famous for. His name, *Shimson*, means 'little sun', but the root of Shimson hints at virility, prompting Jewish writers like Josephus[2] to insist that Samson's name means 'strong'.

His celebrated strength has been used for some unlikely merchandising.

Not only has Samson's name been linked with breakfast cereal, but also with luggage.

The Samsonite Corporation was founded by Jesse Shwayder in 1910. He named one of his early cases 'Samson' and began using the trademark Samsonite in 1941. Samsonite promoted its hard-shell luggage by emphasising its durability with slogans such as 'Strong Enough to Stand On'.

The idea of Samson being a Herculean figure is firmly embedded in our minds.

But what is real strength? Samson was certainly *tough*, but that's not the same as *strong*. And perhaps he wasn't even a body-building, perfect muscleman, which is how he is usually portrayed.

-        -   -   -   -

Jack Bauer is the turbulent hero of *24*, the hyper-tense drama that plays out over a one-day-period of non-stop action. Like Samson, Bauer is captured, but, against all odds, he escapes. He is betrayed by those he trusts, with treachery that leaves the viewer breathless. Bauer has a vast array of skills. Forgive me: he really is a Jack-of-all-trades. But romantically unlucky (most of his love interests end up dead), Jack is a moody, solitary figure, destined to end his days in loneliness. He doesn't smile much.

You don't want to get on the wrong side of Jack. He wreaks cruel vengeance on his enemies, always winning in the end.

He is like Samson, but cooler.

Play a game with me.

Which image do you think of when you hear Samson's name?

Perhaps Jack doesn't come to mind. He's too smooth.

How about Arnold Schwarzenegger, bodybuilder, actor and politician, who glares at the Philistines and, with an Austrian accent, growls, 'I'll be back'?

Charles Atlas, perhaps? Hulk Hogan?

Mr T?

Or Superman, vulnerable only to Kryptonite and Lois Lane?

Whichever image you've chosen, it's unlikely that the 'Samson' in your mind is a spindly computer nerd who avoids beaches because of too much sand-kicking.

Artists throughout history have consistently painted Samson as a beefy giant. Bulging biceps, cavernous chest, a rock-solid six-pack, his laugh a deep-bass roar that made his enemies tremble ...

Rembrandt gave him thighs as thick as tree trunks. Rubens' version was more Braveheart; with a fiery red beard and chiselled, sinewy muscles. His Samson scattered Philistines like skittles; they scampered around him like Lilliputians around Gulliver.

But was he really like that?

The ancient rabbis loved to exaggerate. They taught that Samson's shoulders were 300 feet broad; some said he could carry an object of that size; obviously neither of those claims was meant to be taken literally. Others boasted that Samson could walk from Zorah to Eshtaol with just one stride. It's a distance of about two miles, so that's quite an inside leg. Jewish storytelling endows Samson with superhuman status.

But even the story-weaving rabbis didn't
suggest that Samson had perfect health.

On the contrary.

Some suggested that Samson was disabled.

Put more appropriately, Samson was a disabled person,
but I wanted the starkness of the previous sentence to
impact us. Some rabbis say that Samson's feet were lame.

Forgive me. Like 'crippled', I know that 'lame' is a most
unhelpful word – I only use it to accurately quote them.
Perhaps we shouldn't take the idea too seriously. The
notion might just be another piece of rabbinic folklore.

But it's a winsome, even wonderful, thought
that perhaps Samson wasn't the incredible
hulk (with perfect mobility) after all.

Samson's enemies were desperate to know the *secret*
of his strength. If he was a muscle-bound colossus,
wouldn't that question be redundant? His secret
would be out: he had a gym membership.

I'm not suggesting that Israel's hero was a weedy Clark
Kent figure who became a superhero. Ultimately it's
vital to remember this core truth: Samson was called
to experience strength that came from God. However
rippling his torso, the plan was that his physique was
not to be the ultimate source of his stunning powers.

The mighty man was called to walk in a strength
that came not from his brawn but from the breath
of God within him. Or, to put it another way:

'Not by might nor by power, but by my
Spirit,' says the LORD Almighty.[3]

And that's what I so often forget.

The Christian life is absolutely impossible. If in doubt, scan the Sermon on the Mount.[4] Its demands tower over us, like Everest. We wonder how even to make a start on those seemingly unattainable ideals.

G.K. Chesterton described the sermon as 'impossible stuff'.[5] Another writer, overwhelmed, says the Great Sermon 'spells out the will of God, however unreachable'.[6]

And that's the point.

Humanly speaking, it *is* impossible stuff.

But it's not that God wants us to shrug our shoulders, hoist the white flag of surrender and resign ourselves to sameness. Rather, he wants us to realise *our* secret. And that's Him as our source.

Christianity is not for the morally muscle-bound, a self-help programme with a dash of God here and there. It's a life with the key ingredient for each and every day, forever: Christ.

The Christian life is not just about asking 'What would Jesus do?' Christianity is not just about imitation, but transformation. Without Him, His power, His help, we're beaten before we start.

Jesus makes it plain:

'Apart from me you can do nothing.'[7] That's concise, direct. And quite mystifying.

I know that life is useless and unfruitful without Jesus, that He calls me to 'abide' or 'remain' in Him. But what does that actually mean?

-     -   -   -   -

It's called the Chevy Volt, a hybrid car. Recharging it is simple; you plug it into a standard electrical socket and, the next day, you're able to drive for around 35 miles without using a thimble of petrol.

Once the battery runs out, the car switches over to using regular fuel again.

But the big feature is this: plug in before you drive.

A similar idea about the life of faith has been nestling in my subconscious for years.

Aware that I needed Jesus not only to rescue me but empower me, and hearing that I should be 'being filled with the Holy Spirit', I felt I was like a Chevy Volt. If I was to successfully steer my way through another day in the big bad world, first I needed to plug into a morning quiet time.

This would include worship, prayer and Bible reading in order to charge the cells of my heart and fill me up with Jesus. But the effects of this would only last for a while - certainly a day at the most. The next day I'd need to begin the whole recharging process again. My powerhouse was not a garage, but a prayer time.

To switch the metaphor, it was like one of those old balsa airplanes, where the plastic propeller is driven by an elastic band. Twist the band tighter and tighter and then launch the plane into the air - it then flutters around chaotically for a very little while, before needing to be rewound.

Prayer, reflection and Scripture reading are absolutely vital components of living faith. Spending time with some new friends who embrace an Anglo-Catholic approach to faith, I was impressed - and deeply challenged - by the depth of their spirituality. The wing of the Church that I hail from does not need any more breathless activists who despise solitude and silence.

That said, let's reject too narrow a view of what it means to 'remain' in Christ.

I dwell in Christ not just in solitude but also in community.

I am strengthened and filled with the Holy Spirit afresh by feasting as well as fasting. Nourished by shared stories, energised by caring questions, refreshed by relaxed laughter, I am recharged by belonging.

And I 'remain in Him' as I avoid some of the mistakes that Samson made: being headstrong, rushing into mad decisions. Ignoring good advice. Forgetting solemn vows. Treating prayer as an emergency service, to be used only when in dire need. Refusing to reflect on mistakes. Despising boundaries, rather than accepting them as blessings. Forgetting that actions can have lifelong consequences.

And the biggest mistake of them all: believing that he could make it on his own.

There's the famous moment when Samson gives the secret of his strength away to Delilah.

But there's also an episode when he surely reveals a major reason for his downfall. Having taken on a host of Philistines and won, Samson stands on top of a hill and declares his own triumph:

> 'With a donkey's jaw-bone I have made donkeys of them. With a donkey's jaw-bone I have killed a thousand men.'[8]

What's prominent in his words is *I* – this is a eulogy to self, a monument to his own abilities. There's no reference to God. He celebrates only himself. Even the pagan Philistines were not so foolish as to play that game and gave praise to their god when they finally captured Samson. The fact that theirs was a false god is immaterial: they took the view that they had help beyond themselves.

One of Samson's significant flaws was his independence, his belief in his own strength.

Only when he is at the very end of his life, in terrible torment, does he recognise his source. Milton has Samson humbling himself before God by admitting that his power was not his own:

> God, when he gave me strength, to show withal
> How slight the gift was, hung it in my hair.[9]

But Samson with God - ah, now that was a different story.

Samson *with* God was a head-turner and prompted the Philistines to wonder – what is it that he's got? What's his secret?

Who knows? With God, we can turn heads too and people will ask about *our* secret. Peter, in his first epistle, puts it like this:

> In your hearts set apart Christ as Lord. Always be
> prepared to give an answer to everyone who asks you
> to give the reason for the hope that you have.[10]

But if that is to happen, we should ponder a vital question: is there such a thing as a strong person?

My answer is this:

With One exception, no. Not one.

There's no such thing as a strong person.

Jesus is the obvious exception, although when we use the word 'strong' in connection with Him, we need to take care. Sadly, some think that *strength* means *macho*, obviously in men. A Christian leader recently caused a stir by attacking what he sees as feminised Christianity. Apparently in a desire to see more 'real' men, he insisted that he follows a cage-fighting, high-testosterone Jesus.

> *Some emergent types [want] to recast Jesus as a limp-wrist hippie in a dress with a lot of product in His hair, who drank decaf and made pithy Zen statements about life while shopping for the perfect pair of shoes. In Revelation, Jesus is a prize-fighter with a tattoo down His leg, a sword in His hand and the commitment to make someone bleed. That is the guy I can worship. I cannot worship the hippie, diaper, halo Christ because I cannot worship a guy I can beat up.*[11]

Not only is this a bizarre way to approach worship, but it ignores the reality that Jesus was the lamb of God who *did* allow a few Roman thugs to beat him up. Unfortunately when you think of Jesus being strong in terms of machismo, you start to believe that everyone needs to become Rambo:

> *The problem with our churches today is that the lead pastor is some sissy boy who wears cardigan sweaters, has The Carpenters dialed in on his iPod, gets his hair cut at a salon instead of a barber shop, hasn't been to an Ultimate Fighting match, works out on an elliptical machine instead of going to isolated regions of Russia like in Rocky IV in order to harvest lumber with his teeth ...*[12]

This is a superficial way to think about strength.
Sometimes, those we think of as strong
come disguised as timid, slight souls.

White hair crowns elderly Doris, who sits prim and quiet in the second pew on Sunday, always, always in the same place. She never was a missionary, dodging anacondas in a humid rain forest, nor a wartime nurse just behind the front line, mopping the brows of the dying as shells roared overhead. But don't be fooled, for hers is a stout heart. When cancer stole her breasts and then her husband of fifty years, she was a colossus. For a decade she changed his colostomy bag, never once allowing her nose to wrinkle. It took her three days to summon the courage to view her ravaged, flat-chested frame in a full-length mirror, but she didn't flinch at the sight of those vivid scars. She breathed a prayer of thanks for breath, put her blouse back on and made his tea. She has been strong, a rock in a plaid skirt. And now she sits in that same pew each Sunday, not because it is *her* place, but because it used to be *their* place, together.

But macho foolishness aside, let me say it again:

There's no such thing as a strong person.

Only a person with strengths, who is strong in some areas.

We all know that we all have weaknesses.

But we are also weak *because* we are strong, because our strengths can become components in our weaknesses.

The unwavering, morally solid soul can lack compassion and struggle to show mercy.

The zealous reformer becomes intolerant of others who don't agree with their cause, or don't sacrifice much for it. Their zeal distils into simmering anger and, before long, they lose the ability to win others to their cause. Instead, they alienate.

The tender-hearted giver becomes a pushover for manipulation, a willing target for scammers.

The financially secure despise those who are
lower on the ladder of affluence, dismissing
them as lazy, flawed or even unblessed.

The independent, enterprising type might be
slow to ask for help. Head down, shoulders
square, they march resolutely into oblivion.

The big-picture visionary is often useless on detail. They find it
boring. Vision is cast but flounders because strategy is not set.

And then, whatever our character, we might show
strength today and crumble tomorrow in a different
testing. Some collapse because lethal circumstances
conspire together, with a knockout punch result.

The perception that we're unilaterally strong is deceptive.
People say that we're strong and we believe them. Overly
confident, blinded by their flattery – or deceived by
our lack of self-awareness – we stumble headlong.

Perhaps we are painfully aware of our weaknesses.

But have we ever asked the question: how do my
strengths contribute to my weaknesses?

And perhaps the knowledge that there are no strong people,
only people with strengths, will keep us more alert and awake.

But Israel, years ago, was sound asleep …

Three:
ADDICTIONS COME WITH ANAESTHETIC

'The LORD was with the men of Judah. They took possession of the hill country, but they were unable to drive the people from the plains, because they had iron chariots.'[1]

It's called The Tower of London, although it should be plural: towers.

They mushroomed and there are twenty-one of them. But it all began when William the Conqueror built the White Tower. Taking two decades to construct, the White Tower stands ninety feet high, with walls fifteen feet thick at the bottom, tapering to a 'mere' thickness of eleven feet at the top. Not satisfied with that, our ancestors built a wall around the White Tower's walls. And then other towers and yet another wall to encase the lot. And then another wall. And a moat. They were taking no chances. Originally built as a palace, the Tower became a terrifying prison and a formidable stronghold.

Alcatraz. Nicknamed 'The Rock' and famous for the Birdman and Al Capone, it was a former artillery citadel, designed to protect the city of San Francisco from enemy ships. Its barracks have walls ten feet thick. The prison sits on an island surrounded by the swirling tides of the Bay. I've toured its dour buildings. An atmosphere of hopelessness seems still to pervade it, even though its last prisoner is long gone.

Inmates shivered in tiny, spartan cells, chilled to the bone by sea mist and tormented by laughter and chatter that drifted across the water from glittering parties on the mainland.

So near, so very far. Despair still hangs in the air. It is a stronghold.

Ekron. Together with nearby Gath, it was a fortified city built by the Philistines, a nomadic sea-people originally from Greece, who settled along the eastern Mediterranean coast at the same time as the Israelites settled in the Judean highlands. The Philistines were a tough crowd. Many of them were mercenaries who had worked as hired killers in various wars with Egypt. They were far more sophisticated militarily than the Israelites, having iron swords (the Israelites had only bronze) and three-person chariots: a driver and two warriors. Wearing terrifying headdress, they carried images of their gods into battle. They built sailing boats that could double as battering rams. There were probably about 30,000 of them. Goliath was their most famous son.

These 'sea-people' weren't really a nation, but a coalition of city states each headed by a chief. They took over the Canaanite cities of Gaza, Ashkelon and Ashdod and built Gath and Ekron – which ruled over Timnah, the area where Samson was brought up.

People were terrified of the Philistines. Infamous for their cruelty and methods of torture, one of Israel's most famous kings committed suicide rather than fall into their hands.[2] They worshipped a god called Dagon, who was probably represented by a figure that was half man and half fish and who some believe was appeased by human sacrifice.[3] We become like the god we worship. It seems Dagon loved blood. His followers certainly did.

And so Samson's parents would have lived in the shadow of constant threat and fear. Zorah, their home town, was an outpost settlement right on the dangerous front line with the Philistines, just two miles from Ekron.

That meant living through decades of seething frustration. The area taken over by the Philistines had been allotted to the Israelite tribe of Judah and then Dan in the land distribution agreement hammered out by Joshua.[4] But the Philistines weren't budging. Excavations of Ekron have uncovered a city wall ten feet thick, made of brick. And the Philistines were not content just to defend what they had: they constantly threatened attack, eager to deprive Israel of what she saw as her God-given inheritance. In the Samson story, we'll see that they mounted a huge offensive in response to his destructive handiwork.

By the time Samson was born, it had been this way for decades and frustration had settled down into benign resignation.

It was the way things were.

Nothing to be done.

No prayers to be prayed.

No attempt to repent and renounce their evil ways and turn back to God. They had hardened their hearts, which had become calcified by hopelessness. They were silenced, bowed.

Struggle can prompt prayer. Desperation can make us call upon God with a fervour not known in easier times. That's what had happened previously; twenty years of Canaanite domination had finally nudged Israel to cry out to God for help and He replied by sending them Deborah, the mighty warrior woman.[5] But now, forty long years of powerlessness had come and gone. When nothing changes, year in, year out, we can come to the place where we don't bother to pray any more, not daring to hope lest we are disappointed once again. Children were born and brought up with the knowledge that the Philistines were in charge. Anyone who tried to suggest otherwise was dismissed as a dangerous madman, as Samson himself discovered when a huge and treacherous delegation of his own people went to read him the news and hand him over to the enemy:

> Then three thousand men from Judah went
> down to the cave in the rock of Etam and said to
> Samson, 'Don't you realise that the Philistines are
> rulers over us? What have you done to us?'[6]

They had spent so many days under the shadow of the enemy strongholds, they'd come to believe that this was just how things were.

That's life.

Always was, always will be.

The big story of God had faded into a fairy tale, ancient history, a romantic idea.

Look at how huge those walls are, how thick, how impregnable.

Adjust. Do your best. Survive in their shadow.
Make friends with defeat and settle for sameness.

Of the entire Philistine language, only one word survives, and it describes the reigning chiefs who governed.

Seren.

Lord.

\-   \-   \-   \-   \-

It's an old chestnut. How do you eat an elephant?

One bite at a time.

How do you build a stronghold?

One brick at a time.

Take the stronghold of besetting sin. It all begins quietly.
Temptation comes, not as an enemy, but as a friend,
wooing, seducing, making us an offer we can't refuse.
In the wilderness Jesus didn't encounter a pitch-fork-
waving horned devil, but a smooth, beguiling salesman
with a great line in spin. Sin doesn't strut, it sweet-talks.

As quietly as possible, foundations are being
poured, hewn deep into our soft earth. Elsewhere
I have written about the stronghold of sin:

> *Satan doesn't usually announce his presence with trumpet
> fanfares and vivid night-time apparitions. Such a strategy
> would be far too obvious. Rather, the devil is the master
> of disguise, subtlety and camouflage (2 Cor. 11:14), the
> proverbial salesman who could sell truckloads of sand
> to the Arabs. Satan knows that some fancy footwork
> is required if he is to hoodwink us and thus succeed
> in his task as our prosecuting attorney. So his method
> is quietly to build a sandcastle, a house of thoughts,
> in our minds. With great patience and cunning, with a
> whisper here, a hint there, Satan establishes frontiers
> in our thinking. Day after day, he digs trenches and
> strings barbed wire entanglements in the uncharted
> inner space deep inside our heads. Quietly he weaves
> webs of questions, doubts, fears, suggestions, arguments,
> insinuations. He fires no loud shots – that would alert
> us and put us on guard. Steadily he works towards his
> prize and, at last, the sandcastle becomes a stronghold.[7]*

Slowly, an action becomes a habit, then a vice and finally an addiction. There's no early warning system. No alarm buzzer sounds to warn the late-night internet surfer that they are now in the grip of sexual addiction. No meter reading tells the too-frequent drinker they are now officially an alcoholic.

One brick at a time.

Sin is but one castle under construction.

\- \- \- \- \-

I remember the day that I found out that I was ugly.

It happened at one of those family gatherings where, as a young child, you struggle to make polite conversation with strangers who, apparently, are aunts and uncles. Cups of tea and plates of sandwiches were in hand. My brother was there and his fiancée. I was eleven and a little besotted with her, anxious to please.

'So, you are going to inherit Jeff as a brother-in-law,' said one distant uncle, nodding over at me. 'He does look quite a lot like his older brother, doesn't he?'

She wrinkled her nose in undisguised disdain and looked at me with an expression of disgust: 'Not at all,' she said. 'He looks *nothing* like his brother.' I remember my face flushing red, suddenly ashamed that, apparently, I didn't share my brother's handsome looks.

It seems pathetic for me to even write about it. But that five-second interchange marks a junction in my life, a small, careless moment when nevertheless a verdict was delivered and I accepted it. A careless whisper; the beginning of a trench dug and a foundation poured.

One brick at a time.

—   —   —   —   —

All this talk of stealth shouldn't imply that
strongholds sit quietly in our lives.

Strongholds are built quietly but then shout their
presence. Taunt would be a better description.
That's what Philistines are good at.

Saul found that out when he spent six futile weeks
trying to solve the Goliath problem. The famous giant,
with a huge head and a mouth to match, taunted
the king and his trembling people every day.

> Goliath stood and shouted to the ranks of Israel, 'Why do
> you come out and line up for battle? Am I not a Philistine,
> and are you not the servants of Saul? Choose a man and
> have him come down to me. If he is able to fight and kill me,
> we will become your subjects; but if I overcome him and kill
> him, you will become our subjects and serve us.' Then the
> Philistine said, 'This day I defy the ranks of Israel! Give me a
> man and let us fight each other.' On hearing the Philistine's
> words, Saul and all the Israelites were dismayed and terrified.[8]

Milton, in his *Samson Agonistes*, takes some liberties with the
story, but does well to create an extra biblical character called
Harapha, a Philistine giant. He visits the captive Samson and
taunts him, accusing him of all kinds of evil: revolt, murder
and theft. Harapha points out that Samson is worthless, a
warrior tamed by the razor that was used to cut his hair:

> No worthy match
> For valor to assail, nor by the sword
> Of noble warrior
> But by the barber's razor best subdued.[9]

THERE ARE NO STRONG PEOPLE

In Milton, the blind Samson is able to send
Harapha packing before he dies.

Like a huge castle that blights the horizon, the presence of a stronghold in our lives mocks us:

You're not really a Christian at all, are you?

Where's your faith now?

What's the point in trying?

And the taunting erodes our hope.

Ed Silvoso has said 'A stronghold is a mind-set impregnated with hopelessness that causes us to accept as unchangeable situations that we know are contrary to the will of God'.[10]

We forget that we have power, that we
can fight back. Paul reminds us:

> *The weapons we fight with are not the weapons of the world. On the contrary, they have divine power to demolish strongholds. We demolish arguments and every pretension that sets itself up against the knowledge of God and we take captive every thought to make it obedient to Christ.*[11]

Meanwhile, back in Zorah, life continued as usual,
the same nervous drudgery, the daily grind.

But God had other plans.

-      -   -   -   -

God is impatient.

Okay, one writer softens this statement a little, talking about 'Yahweh's impatient grace'.[12] But the idea is the same. There are times when God tires of waiting around for His people to wake up and so, even though no one's praying and hope and expectation are in short supply, God steps in.

Moses experienced this:

'You have stayed long enough at this mountain. Break camp ...'[13]

So did Joshua.

'Moses my servant is dead. Now then, you and all these people, get ready ...'[14]

Similar language was used by the angel who visited the woman who would bear Samson. In the Hebrew text, there's a sense of haste as the angel gives instructions on how the child should be brought up.

It's as if the angel is excited. On tiptoes. Light was about to break into darkness. A little sun, *Shimson*, was coming.

God is long-suffering. Thankfully, He is slow to anger. But when He sees us cowering, intimidated by strongholds, surrounded by unused weapons, He is impatient to see us free.

Perhaps that's not the picture of God that we're used to: a God who hops from one foot to another. Who looks at His watch. And tut-tuts.

Perhaps our picture of God makes Him a plodder, slow, painfully methodical.

Three thousand years ago, no one was praying, but God was noticing and was about to take action.

Wake up, Israel.

What about us?

Four:
OUR DEEPEST NEED IS TO BE KNOWN

'I'd rather be hated for who I am, rather than loved for who I am not.' – Kurt Cobain[1]

I used to love the dodgems.

They were the highlight of the funfair for me. Shiny little cars in gaudy reds, blues and golds, powered by a sparking overhead electric grid, surreal because of their lacquered, gold-flake finish. Lined with rubber bumpers, the whole idea was to twirl around and bump other cars as you did. To avoid being bumped yourself, you dodged them – hence, dodgems.

But now bumping has been taken out of the dodgems; suffocating health and safety fears have ended the fun. A student in Northern Ireland was awarded €7,000 after being struck by a 'rogue driver' on the dodgems in County Donegal in 2009.

And so now Butlins have decided that 'excessive bumping' will no longer be tolerated. Ironically Sir Billy Butlin, who founded the company, was responsible for bringing dodgems to the UK from America in 1923.

It's ironic. We live in a sue-happy, blame culture.

And yet, at the same time, a sense of personal responsibility seems to be at an all-time low. Comedian and singer Anna Russell lampoons our tendency to pass the proverbial buck:

I went to my psychiatrist to be psychoanalysed

To find out why I killed the cat and
blackened my husband's eyes.

He laid me on a downy couch to see what he could find,

And here is what he dredged up from
my subconscious mind:

When I was one, my mommie hid my dolly in a trunk,

And so it follows naturally that I am always drunk.

When I was two, I saw my father kiss the maid one day,

And that is why I suffer now from kleptomania.

At three, I had the feeling of ambivalence
towards my brothers,

And so it follows naturally I poison all my lovers.

But I am happy; now I've learned the lesson this has taught;

That everything I do that's wrong is someone else's fault.[2]

So what has this to do with Samson and his childhood home?
I'm not about to suggest that Samson was just a hapless
victim of his upbringing and therefore not responsible
for his own well-documented follies. Ultimately, he made
his choices – and, whatever our histories, so do we.

But those choices were surely shaped by his nurture
– and many writers and commentators have observed
that his was not a happy home. On the contrary, a close
look at how Scripture describes his parents' interaction
reveals crackling tensions in their marriage.

The point is not that we use our past to excuse ourselves,
but that we seek to understand ourselves more as we

consider where we've come from. Perhaps our personal history sets us up for disaster long before any tempter stops by. To know where we have been helps us to understand who and where we are. In Samson's case, not only was he born into a home that was fractured by disappointment and despair, but another, rather surprising, factor contributed to his ultimate collapse: he was orphaned by his own calling. He was chosen by God, but perhaps there was a dark side to that beautiful destiny. From the womb, he belonged to God and God's purposes. And perhaps that meant that, in his parents' eyes, he never really belonged to *them*.

-        -   -   -   -

Question. What is the etiquette for entertaining visiting angels?

Answer: Don't be frightened (the usual response is blind terror), don't argue (humans usually do, especially when the angel brings stunningly good news), stop talking and listen (the rustle of angelic wings normally prompts an inordinate amount of blabbering).

Based on what usually happens when angels bump into humans, Samson's mother did rather well. But the encounter with the 'man of God' and the resulting exchange between husband and wife reveal some seismic fractures in their marriage.

As we zoom in on an Israelite family, don't be tempted, as some commentators have, to romanticise them and turn them into faith-filled heroes.

Israel was far from God at this time; Samson's parents lived in a culture where the real God had been relentlessly rejected. They were a product of their culture. When Manoah and his wife talk about God, they don't call him *Yahweh*, but *Elohim*,

the generic designation for deity (and the name that, as we'll
see, Samson would often use for God). At best, these two had
a vague notion of the divine - someone who probably existed,
but whose existence made little difference to their days. Of
course, that neutered notion about God is very prevalent
today. But for them, everything was about to change.

Cataclysmically.

-        -   -   -   -

She would have hated the sound of the word and yet
it had become as familiar as her name. *Akhara*.

Barren one.

In her era, barrenness meant even more than the crushing
despair experienced by childless parents today. Childlessness
brought acute social stigma as well. The popular belief was that
childless couples were being punished for offending the gods
who controlled reproduction. In Israel, children were thought to
be a sign of the blessing of God and so barrenness was a sign of
divine displeasure, His curse. Like a rain cloud that would never
shift, heartache and shame had hung over Samson's mother
and her husband for years. There were practical issues created
by barrenness too: without offspring to care for them, childless
parents approached their twilight years with justified fear.

Akhara.

It's devastating when people name us according
to our most obvious challenge.

The blind guy.

Him in the wheelchair.

The Down's syndrome kid.

Our own name fades and, when we're dubbed according
to our disability, our struggle is scrawled all over us.
We fear that no one sees
the person that is really us:
their superficial scanning
means that they only see a
tiny part of who we are.

Akhara.

—   —   —   —   —

It's awkward to say it, but the angel seemed quite
brutal. He addresses her by telling her what she
knew too well: *you are sterile and childless.*

She probably thought: thanks very much.
Do you think I need any reminder?

Perhaps the terse announcement brought some helpful clarity.

You are sterile.

What childless couple hasn't wondered: which of us is
the problem? Is a dead womb or lacklustre sperm to
blame for our barrenness? Various parts of the Midrash,[3]
the collections of expository comments on the Hebrew
texts,[4] say that there was a quarrel between the two
of them regarding the cause of their childlessness.

But now, if this remarkable stranger was to be believed,
at last she knew. If she had secretly blamed her husband,
then she'd been wrong. Had she despised him for not
giving her the child she so desperately wanted?

Perhaps for too many long years she had hoped and dreamed and had finally decided to shelve her hopes for good. But now – double joy! Not only is she going to have a child, but a male child at that – again, a major bonus in the culture of the day.

But how quickly did the bubble of joy linger, before it was burst by another realisation that would dawn in her mind?

She is going to have a son, but, in a way, she will never really have a son. With a sentence, a baby is given to her and then snatched away by the news of his calling. That son to be hers was nationalised in the womb.

He is to be Israel's son. God's agent. Not just her longed-for darling.

And, in the angel's announcement, already a mother's prerogative is being overruled.

Somebody else is telling her how the boy should be brought up. All those tiny decisions mothers love to make are suddenly being overruled by a stranger. She is, as one writer puts it bleakly, 'a surrogate mother for God's plans'.[5] Did she feel that she was carrying a foreigner in her womb? Perhaps his impending potential greatness made her feel inadequate, like the mother of Andrei Sakharov, the genius physicist, who lamented: 'Sometimes I feel like a chicken who gave birth to an eagle.'[6]

Did the special child to be born alienate her because she felt so very ordinary?

She rushes to tell her husband – but then weaves intrigue into the announcement, not because of what she says, but how she says it - and what she keeps to herself. Samson is but a speck in the womb, but already secrets are forming.

The news of a sudden pregnancy was always going to provoke suspicion; but a close look at the language she used suggests that's exactly what she wanted. She seems to want her husband to be on edge; she deliberately provokes him. When she says 'a man of God came to me' she picks a word that usually referred to copulation. Did she want him to be anxious, fearful about what had really happened? Why? What resentment simmered beneath the surface? If there was true love between them, then she would never have wanted this wonderful news to be spoiled by fear and intrigue.

The 'man of God' is nameless, perhaps compounding Manoah's suspicion.

I've been with a man.

What's his name?

I don't know.

Where's he from?

I don't know.

Why don't you know?

I didn't ask him and he didn't tell me.

I'm pregnant.

If Manoah didn't have any qualms about her story (which is unlikely), then others have certainly considered her explanation and wondered. Commentators and writers down the ages have wrinkled their noses and rolled their eyes.

Yeah, right, an angel stopped by.

That explains everything. Makes perfect sense. Not.

Vladimir Jabotinsky, in his classic novel *Samson the Nazarite* (which formed the basis of Cecil B. de Mille's classic film *Samson and Delilah*), departs from the biblical narrative and suggests that a liaison between Samson's mother and a very real flesh-and-blood Philistine was the cause of the sudden conception.[7]

But the conversation between the woman and her husband gets even more odd.

She speaks of her son's vow that will be in effect until his dying day. It's a strange time to talk of death – especially as the angel made no mention of this. Samson's mother is weaving her own subconscious thoughts and fears into the report for her husband. As we'll see, Nazirite vows were usually taken voluntarily for a specific time span.

What mother rushes to think about the death of her child, even before he's been born? Is the realisation dawning on her that this was good news and perhaps terrible news?

She was supposed to feel so honoured, so privileged: her son would grow up to become a national figure. But that nation was living under the heel of the fearsome Philistines. And so his calling would inevitably mean trouble. There would be battles to fight. Politics to navigate, misunderstandings to negotiate. And it would all most likely end with a terrible death for her unborn son. The 'man of God' had said that he would begin to deliver Israel: why only a *beginning*? Would his life be snuffed out too early, meaning that he could never finish what he had started? Was her unborn shuffling to a premature death already, his days numbered before he had even left the womb?

She tells her husband what she's decided he needs to know, but leaves out the two most important pieces of information: that her son will never take a razor to his head and that he will be a deliverer of Israel. Did she want to cherish this revelation for herself, hold it close to her heart? Was the last person she sought to share her earth-shattering secret with her own husband?

For whatever reason, she becomes a censor, editing out the most vital news about the child.

She becomes a woman with a blockbuster secret.

Like mother, like son, as Samson's story will show.

-      -   -   -   -

Look at him, this Manoah.

The suddenly expectant father.

He's sullen, distant, unmoved. There's no joy, no celebration. Perhaps his eyes are narrowed, his brow furrowed. He wants to know more. To his credit, he prays and is heard, which is gracious, because his prayer voices suspicion.

He asks for more information about how to bring up the child. Why? The Nazirite rules were clear enough. It seems that he wants to gain control of the situation; irritated that some stranger – even a man sent from God – has been consorting with his wife, he tries to get a grip by asking questions that don't need an answer: insecure blustering. Is he resentful, jealous and hungry to take the reins of power back in his own home?

He prays and God answers, but not in the way that he wants. On the contrary. The man of God has another solitary conversation with *Akhara* again. Manoah's excluded once more.

It looks like some taunting is going on, her second meeting with a stranger acting like salt in Manoah's wounds.

Breathless from the second encounter, she runs to find her husband and, giddy, she tells him: *he's here again!*

She turns and dashes back to the field of dreams
where the man of God waits. But her husband trudges
behind, a strange portrait in Near Eastern culture, when
men invariably led the way. Ancient rabbis chastise
Manoah and call him an *am ha'aretz*, an ignoramus,
for lolloping along after his wife as he did.

There's something weary, reluctant, about his gait.
The words used describe slow, heavy movements.
No one consulted him about this plan: he was simply
informed of a *fait accompli*. And now, there's been a
second meeting with the 'man of God' for his wife.

Manoah's conversation with the angel is straight to the point,
awkward, even embarrassing. The angel seemed rather
more terse, or at least curt. Do angels have off days?

Manoah speaks of 'the boy that is to be born', as if he is already
resigned to the idea that his son will never really be just his
son: the child has come as a result of the visit of a passing
stranger. Angel or infidel, it still meant that the child was not
just the fruit of their marriage. A visitor is involved, an invader.

Not that Manoah quickly concludes that this
was an angel. He seems dim-witted.

Sceptical and jumpy.

To revisit an earlier question, what's the
etiquette when an angel shows up?

According to Manoah, you ask him for ID.

Proof of identity.

And then, still unaware that he is talking to a messenger of
God - or perhaps God Himself - he ambles into convention,
offering the stranger a meal, which again is curtly refused.

A sacrifice follows. And a terrifying ignition of fire. The angel is gone and, only as he goes, does Manoah realise who it was that he was just talking to. But his blundering continues, as he bleats out that he and his wife are surely going to die because of this encounter. It's left to his wife to explain that he is safe.

In painting this scene Rembrandt favours Manoah's wife, in his *Sacrifice of Manoah*. At first glance Manoah appears 'slumped facedown like a sack of potatoes'.[8] His wife sits upright, seeing, understanding, focused. Later, when it is time for Samson to seek a bride, he asks his father and mother about it. Culture would usually insist that this was men's talk. But not with Manoah. No wonder one writer dubs him, perhaps a little too unkindly, 'that dolt of a husband'.[9] Another is even more disparaging, calling him comical, obtuse, a bumbling fool.[10]

Later, when the child is born, we're specifically told that his *mother* gave him the name Samson. While either parent could decide a name in ancient Israel (and more often women, not men, chose the name), in context, the writer wants us to know: Samson's mother rules the roost. She is the strong character and Manoah is marginalised even further.

The choice of the name *Samson* might be significant too. We've already seen that Samson, *Shimson*, meant little sun, or, as one commentator has it, 'sunny boy'. Perhaps Manoah's wife chose that name because the birth of this child, even this strange, otherworldly child, brought a ray of sunshine to her otherwise dull life, harnessed as she was, if Manoah's harsh critics are to be believed, to such a feckless husband.

Samson. Shimson.

The sunshine of her life.

Sunny boy grows to be like his mother: keeping his cards close to his chest; going wandering, but saying nothing.

Epic events happen to the young Samson, but he doesn't tell his parents. He kills a lion with his bare hands and stays quiet. He gives them honey from the carcass, but doesn't tell them where it came from. And his parents seem to stay out of the loop. Even when God uses Samson's headstrong temperament to get His will done, the blunt verdict on his parents is this: *they did not know.* A massive chasm widens between them and their odd son, their one and only. Their supposed sunshine is on a distant horizon.

Perhaps the confusion that his mother felt at the news of his call made her manipulative, overprotective – or the opposite: distant and detached. It appears that she doesn't attend her own son's wedding. Perhaps she can't bear the thought of another woman taking her place. And, as for his father, how could he ever understand what Samson was to feel? The first time we hear a conversation between Samson and his parents, he is telling them what to do and he doesn't take no for an answer. Samson is a loner. No one really knows him. Nobody is close.

-       -   -   -   -

There are some who would suggest that Samson was not just mildly affected by his childhood, but that he was mentally ill, suffering from the earliest recorded case of Anti-Social Personality Disorder (ASPD). The BBC reported[11] that Dr Eric Altschuler, from the University of California, in San Diego, stated in *New Scientist* magazine that in today's society Samson would be seen to have ASPD, because he was 'a bit of a thug'. He said he had gone back to his Bible and begun to reappraise Samson in a totally new light. Altschuler came to his conclusions after revisiting the story that had been familiar to him from childhood days:

I knew the story of Samson from when I was a kid. I re-read the story and the general impression was that he was a strong man, but I found that he was anti-social. When I used to go to Sunday school I thought he was good and led the battles. But he starts the fights and the battles. Appreciation of the diagnosis of ASPD for Samson may not only help us to better understand the Biblical story, but it also may increase our understanding and awareness of instances when a leader has ASPD.[12]

Dr Altschuler said that the fact that Samson told Delilah (a woman who had already tried to kill him three times) the secret of his strength shows that he was deliberately self-destructive. According to Altschuler, Samson shows no fewer than six out of the seven characteristics of ASPD.

He is impulsive, has an inability to conform to social norms and is deceitful; he sets things on fire, tortures animals, steals and bullies.

-      -   -   -   -

Whatever we might think about Samson's mental health, this much is definite: he was a loner and was unwilling - or unable - to act in concert with his own people, preferring to function solo, a maverick.

Loners don't really know people. And that means that they are not known. And surely that was a huge problem for Samson.

What is it that all women and men want, whoever they are?

Fast forward the story to that most famous episode, when Samson is finally betrayed by his Delilah.

Just as Samson's sins tend to write the headlines over his life, so Delilah's wicked treachery tends to dominate this scene. But peer closer.

Samson sleeps, cradled in the lap of his lover. He is nestled in a woman's arms; she perhaps strokes his head and whispers sweet nothings, just as his mother had done many years before hoping for an intimate bond with her strange, growing child.

On Delilah's lap, the turbulent soul is resting at last, slumber allowing him a few minutes escape from the restlessness that has wracked his every waking moment.

And he is known. His secret has been shared, his soul laid bare to one that he believed to be trustworthy.

Isn't this a portrait of what we all long for? To be safe and to be known.

In the Old Testament, we read that a man *knew* his wife, a term that describes their sexual union. Far more than just a mechanical cohabiting, or a means of procreation, sex is a gift enabling exploration, acceptance, tenderness and utter vulnerability in our nakedness. That's why sex without intimacy and commitment is such a cheap, unsatisfying imitation.

But intimacy is obviously not just expressed sexually. Most of us want others to join themselves to the real us that lives just beneath our skin; to know our ridiculous hopes, even our seedy secrets, our scabs and wounds. We don't want people to love or like us for who they *think* we are, but for who we really are.

Samson must have lived bewildered by the news of his strange conception and his early experiences of Spirit-fuelled strength and inward compulsion. Perhaps, with Delilah, he finally felt that he could tell all, be himself without fear, give her everything, even the secret behind his powerful exploits.

He could let someone else in, give her his heart and break the solitary confinement of his calling. And so, for once, he rests.

I cannot put it more beautifully than
Hebrew writer David Grossman:

> Samson withdraws into his childish, almost infantile self,
> disarmed of the violence, madness and passion that
> have confounded and ruined his life. This is, of course,
> also the moment when his fate is sealed, for Delilah
> is clutching his hair and the razor and the Philistines
> outside are already relishing their victory. In another
> moment his eyes will be plucked out and his power
> extinguished. Soon he will be thrown into prison and
> his days will be ended. Yet it is now, perhaps for the first
> time in his life, that he finds repose. Here, in the very
> heart of the cruel perfidy that he had surely expected
> all along, he is finally granted perfect peace, a release
> from himself and the stormy dramas of his life.[13]

For much of his life, Samson wasn't known. Others
help us to know who we are. And that raises the
possibility of a terrible thought: did Samson even
know that he was called to be a deliverer of Israel?
Saviours need to know that they are saviours.

But only one time in his life does Samson talk about being a
Nazirite - and that was in his disastrous confession to Delilah.
And then, he never mentions anything about a national
call as deliverer. He had received no personal calling - that
had come through his parents, specifically his mother.

Did they ever tell him the full truth about his origins - or, more
importantly, did Samson's mother, who didn't even let her
husband in on the full story, ever get around to telling Samson?
Did she withhold the information, hoping that, in doing so,
she might be able to keep her little sunshine all for herself?

Five:
GOD IS LOOKING FOR STRANGE PEOPLE

'Propaganda is a truly terrible weapon in
the hands of an expert.' – Adolf Hitler[1]

It was the smell of leather that prompted my surprising reaction.

I didn't know whether to cry, or throw up. Or both.

Leather: usually one of my favourite smells.

The scent of the ancient. A hint of it and I am suddenly
in an ornate study in an old English house. There's a
lingering aroma of burned logs from the charcoal ashes
in the stone fireplace. Long-dead nobles stare down at me
from the old masters that hang on oak-panelled walls.

There is a huge pedestal desk, an
expensive fountain pen atop it.

And, the final masterpiece: two sumptuous
brown leather chairs, worn by the years, yet
all the more beautiful for their age.

Leather: the scent of newness. A luxury car, loaded
with refinement, elegance, built for comfort.

Leather: nauseating here.

We were visiting the National Holocaust
Museum in Washington DC.

The Museum is in turn brilliant, sickening,
arresting and harrowing.

We recoiled at the grainy black-and-white footage of Jews
being shot in the head and then kicked into shallow graves
that they had just dug for themselves, some of them probably
still alive as they tumbled in, limbs chaotically all akimbo.

We had stood silently in one of the old *Guterwagans*, the
railway cars used to transport thousands to Auschwitz
who were to be greeted by the lying sign over the
entry gate: *Arbeit Macht Frei.* 'Work makes freedom.'

We stared at the reconstructed ovens in
which millions were turned to ash.

But it was the last display that turned my heart and stomach.
A glass trough, maybe twenty feet in length, was filled
with shoes. Hundreds, perhaps thousands, of shoes.

They were found piled high in the death camps, snatched
from Jews who wouldn't be needing them any more.

I leaned over the trough and breathed in deeply
and inhaled the smell of those old leather shoes and
suddenly knew in a way that I had not known before,
in a way that the photographs and films and statistics
couldn't tell me: real people died. Six million of them.

Here were their shoes.

The haunting question posed by the exhibition – and by
that smell of leather – was this: how did the Nazi regime so
effectively capture the minds of so many of the German people,
so that the Jewish population could be so mercilessly hounded,
vilified and ultimately herded into gas chambers disguised as
shower blocks, like lambs to the slaughter? Even if the majority
of the German public were oblivious to what was going

on behind the electrified barbed wire of the concentration camps, some *did* know. And six million people *were* arrested and uprooted from their communities, just because of their ethnicity. A terrible tide of anti-Semitism had been rising during the thirties, so the Nazis did not have to invent the notion of the 'evil within' that was the Jewish people – they just had to harness that growing mood of hatred. How did they do that?

The answer is simple and complex: propaganda.

Propagation is what happens when flora and fauna reproduce. Ironically, it was the Christian Church that first started to use the term to describe the dissemination of ideas. A special division was created within the Roman Catholic Church in the seventeenth century, in an effort to combat the rising tide of Protestantism. It was called the *propaganda fide*.

Soon others caught on to the deliberate manipulation of ideas that is propaganda – especially after World War One, which many believe was won not by bullets but by the continuing selling of the idea of peace that sapped the energy of German fighting troops. Post-World-War-One Germany lamented the lack of their own propaganda machinery. Some politicians and scholars of propaganda urged Germans to learn from the victors. Among these was a former German soldier and leader of an obscure right-wing extremist party in Bavaria. His name was Adolf Hitler.

Nazi propagandists systematically eliminated the free exchange of ideas, used terror and controlled the media, allowing their leaders a free rein to commit aggression, mass murder and genocide. Unlike education, which seeks to encourage critical thinking and independent judgment, propaganda is monochrome: the propagandist transmits only information geared to strengthen his or her case and consciously omits detrimental information.

The relentless force of manipulative ideas led to terrified children screaming for their parents, only to discover that they too were being herded towards the makeshift gas chambers. Propaganda paved the way.

But propaganda only works because we are creatures of the herd.

We like to act together.

We want to fit in, sometimes with devastating results.

- - - - -

It's called an informational cascade. And it works for the holocaust, or for the sale of hairspray; the same power is at work in the tragic and the trivial.

Take the world of fashion, for example. Someone, somewhere, says 'this is cool', and hawks the notion to us via costly marketing and advertising; others start to buy the idea and we, eager to fit in, comply and surrender up our credit cards. A trend has been set. We follow it, lemming-like, sometimes over the cliff of bad taste, as anyone who has lived through the decade - and the fashions - of the seventies knows.

An informational cascade happens when you watch what I do and listen to what I say and then make the exact same choices I have made, even though you may think that I'm wrong. We tend to think that the crowd is right and, if we dissent, that we're probably misguided, out of line.

Thus we fit in, we conform. Even when the crowd, or an entire nation, is utterly wrong, we hesitate to break step. Non-conformity demands great confidence and greater courage.

But those who follow Christ are called to vacate the herd.

To be different.

And that's what Samson was called to be: the stranger in town, odd because of God.

Or, to put it more specifically, the man with untamed hair. The Nazirite.

\-   \-   \-   \-   \-

Perhaps Samson resented the vow.

After all, he'd never had any choice in the matter. His mother would have told him about the visit of the man of God – but he had never bumped into any angels himself.

Who knows?

Perhaps he wondered at times if his mother had been deluded by a hyperactive imagination. Or if it was all simply her manipulative attempt to tame him. He would have grown up watching his strong-willed mother and his shrinking violet of a father and perhaps wondered if she was just that way around everybody, using her cleverness to get others to do things her way.

Listen, sunny boy, before you were born, God told me ...

Right, Ma. Sure He did.

Did he feel sealed in by the choices of others – trapped by a vow that took effect before he even took his first breath and one that would only end when he drew his last?

No way out of that, then ...

The Nazirite vow was always taken as a choice, a free-will decision. Like a decision to fast for a while, the vow was supposed to be a voluntary, seasonal act. Women as well as men could decide to abstain from alcohol (or from eating any products that came from grapes) for a set time. They would leave their hair uncut and diligently avoid any contact with a dead body. Usually lasting around thirty days, anyone could begin the period of the vow by simply saying 'me too' as a Nazirite walked by.

And so perhaps he chafed at the bit that was the vow.

Certainly he seemed to do everything to ignore it.

He threw a lengthy drinking party to celebrate his marriage: hardly the behaviour usually anticipated from someone pledged to be a lifelong total abstainer.

And, as we'll see, Samson spent his life pushing boundaries.

He was forever playing with ropes, vines, knots and gates.

Like an emotional Houdini, it's as if Samson wanted to endlessly prove: you can't tie me up or down.

Arrest me and tie me with new ropes.

Look! I broke free …

Bind me with vines, Delilah. Lash my hair to a weaver's loom if you like. I'm Samson the escapologist.

Do your worst, Philistines.

I'll rent one of your prostitutes for an hour or so and then, when you come after me, not only will I escape through the city gates, but I'll carry the gates and posts off with me too.

It's all rather sad.

Much of the time, Samson used his uncommon
strength to act like any other careless, self-indulgent
man. To test the boundaries and breach them.

To be one of the boys. Just like the rest.

-        -   -   -   -

Earlier I asked if it might be possible that Samson never
actually knew that he was called to begin the deliverance
of Israel – and that's one reason that he ignored (or at least
treated lightly) the call to be different. At the very least perhaps
he never knew quite *why* he was called to be different.

His own people turned against him, betrayed him
and tried to hand him over to the Philistines.

But, although he broke free, he made no speech to his
people. There was no call to arms, no rallying cry.

Nothing.

No wonder one scholar says,

> *Samson seems totally oblivious to what*
> *God was trying to do through him.*[2]

Another: 'Israel failed to recognise Samson as their God-
given deliverer and Samson was confused about his role
in life ... in the story to follow Samson never gives any
indication he understood himself to be Israel's deliverer.'[3]

Or maybe he did once know what his role was, but
gradually forgot the calling and was left with the hollow
shell that was the vow. And once he forgot the reason
for the vow, it became an irksome, prohibitive chain
around his soul, another fetter to escape from.

You can't tie me down.

Empty vows.

Rules without purpose.

Religion does that.

We embrace a value, then the value creates a choice, a choice becomes a discipline and then a discipline becomes a rule.

After a while, the value fades, but the rule remains. And we've forgotten the reason that the rule was made in the first place.

For Samson, the purpose of God was simple: he was called to be a stranger, a soul that stood out from the crowd, a walking wake-up call. He was called to be a sign and a wonder.

Perhaps that's one reason why it mattered that he didn't cut his hair and that the cutting of it would be the last straw, the moment when God's power left him. There was no magic power in those locks.

But his hair was the sign and seal of his being set apart for the purposes of God. As one writer says, 'Samson's locks were a visible word, proclaiming to friend and foe alike that he was set apart to the Lord.'[4]

Samson's hair was only the sign of his strength, not the source of it.

But, in allowing his hair to be cut, Samson turns his back totally on living as a *nazir*; he is no longer distinctive in any way, he has finally joined the crowd.

But he was always called to be utterly different.

Head turning.

And so are we.

Repeatedly, in his epistles, Peter calls us to be 'strangers'. This is not a call to be strange, which is a relief, because I've met a few Christians who don't need any further encouragement in that direction. But we are required to resist the pressure to go with the flow: whatever our tradition, we are all called, at heart, to be nonconformists. This is no superficial thing, but cuts deep. We are called to strange priorities, ambitions, hopes and everyday values. To love in the face of spite; to serve expecting nothing in return; to trust in the valley of pain and continue heavenward when heaven is silent. To be different.

Saying yes to Christ will often mean saying no to the subtle and sometimes crass suggestions that we just settle down and fit in.

The strange life.

Living as strangers, yet named as friends of God.

Book Two
THE RIDDLER

He grew and the LORD blessed him, and the Spirit of the LORD began to stir him while he was in Mahaneh Dan, between Zorah and Eshtaol.

Samson went down to Timnah and saw there a young Philistine woman. When he returned, he said to his father and mother, 'I have seen a Philistine woman in Timnah; now get her for me as my wife.'

His father and mother replied, 'Isn't there an acceptable woman among your relatives or among all our people? Must you go to the uncircumcised Philistines to get a wife?'

But Samson said to his father, 'Get her for me. She's the right one for me.' (His parents did not know that this was from the LORD, who was seeking an occasion to confront the Philistines; for at that time they were ruling over Israel.) Samson went down to Timnah together with his father and mother. As they approached the vineyards of Timnah, suddenly a young lion came roaring towards him. The Spirit of the LORD came upon him in power so that he tore the lion apart with his bare hands as he might have torn a young goat. But he told neither his father nor his mother what he had done. Then he went down and talked with the woman, and he liked her.

Some time later, when he went back to marry her, he turned aside to look at the lion's carcass. In it was a swarm of bees and some honey, which he scooped out with his hands and ate as he went along. When he rejoined his parents, he gave them some, and they too ate it. But he did not tell them that he had taken the honey from the lion's carcass.

Now his father went down to see the woman. And Samson made a feast there, as was customary for bridegrooms. When he appeared, he was given thirty companions.

'Let me tell you a riddle,' Samson said to them. 'If you can give me the answer within the seven days of the feast, I will give you thirty linen garments and thirty sets of clothes. If you can't tell me the answer, you must give me thirty linen garments and thirty sets of clothes.'

'Tell us your riddle,' they said. 'Let's hear it.'

He replied,

'Out of the eater, something to eat;

out of the strong, something sweet.'

For three days they could not give the answer.

On the fourth day, they said to Samson's wife, 'Coax your husband into explaining the riddle for us, or we will burn you and your father's household to death. Did you invite us here to rob us?'

Then Samson's wife threw herself on him, sobbing, 'You hate me! You don't really love me. You've given my people a riddle, but you haven't told me the answer.'

'I haven't even explained it to my father or mother,' he replied, 'so why should I explain it to you?' She cried the whole seven days of the feast. So on the seventh day he finally told her, because she continued to press him. She in turn explained the riddle to her people.

Before sunset on the seventh day the men of the town said to him,

'What is sweeter than honey?

What is stronger than a lion?'

Samson said to them,

'If you had not ploughed with my heifer,

you would not have solved my riddle.'

Then the Spirit of the LORD came upon him in power. He went down to Ashkelon, struck down thirty of their men, stripped them of their belongings and gave their clothes to those who had explained the riddle. Burning with anger, he went up to his father's house. And Samson's wife was given to the friend who had attended him at his wedding.[1]

Six:
BLESSED ARE THE AGITATED, FOR THEY SHALL NEVER BE SATISFIED

'Those who believe they believe in God, but without passion in the heart, without anguish of mind, without uncertainty, without doubt and even at times without despair, believe only in the idea of God and not in God Himself.' – Madeleine L'Engle[1]

'If you're seeking happiness, don't choose Christianity, choose port wine.' – C.S. Lewis[2]

'We must fight the temptation to treat our faith the way we treat our careers – as a source of entertainment, fulfillment and happiness ... we must rely on more than cheerful tunes, easy answers and happy smiles.' – Chuck Colson[3]

The bride is beautiful, picture-perfect for her dream day.

Her hair is a sculptured masterpiece, impossibly held in place. Her dress shimmers, snowy white, stunning.

She has longed for this moment. And her longing continues.

Glancing at the clock for the fifth time that minute, her impatient fidgeting has turned to anxious striding up and down now. She stops and glances over at the waiting priest, hoping to find some reassurance in his eyes.

When will he be here? Is he coming?

She is agitated. Impatient. She cranes her neck. Is that him at last?

This is the posture of the healthy Church: a bride desperate for her bridegroom, agitated until He arrives.

But she is unlike any other bride who has ever stood before an altar, because her ache is not just for herself and her husband-to-be, for their honeymoon and the lifelong union to follow. The Church yells desperately, 'Come back, Lord Jesus!', because she is moved and troubled about so much that continues to go terribly wrong while she waits for the fullness of His coming and His kingdom.

Until He comes at last, children's bellies will still ache and distend and some will close their eyes in sleep tonight, still hungry, never to wake again. Come on, Jesus. Come back.

Narrow-eyed dictators still oppress, mercilessly destroying their detractors in state-sanctioned brutality. Is that You, Lord? Will You please come back and finally establish and consummate Your reign?

Young women are trafficked, sold like chattels, used and passed around by men with filthy bodies and hearts and then tossed aside like broken, unwanted dolls. Come back, Lord.

Everything is not as it should be, and won't be, until the King comes.

And so, the bride, the healthy Church, waits and works and wonders, but is ultimately agitated to see His face at last ...

Blessed are the agitated.

It's the plight of the people who live between two ages: the kingdom that is and the kingdom yet to come. This is the destiny of any who encounter the agitating Spirit of God, who shakes and unsettles us and plants within us an insatiable thirst for change.

Surely this was Samson's plight, too.

-      -   -   -   -

The Lord blessed him.

He is the only one of Israel's judges of whom that is said, which is remarkable when we consider how his life turned out.

The Lord blessed him.

Other judges were said to be clothed with God's Spirit,[4] but only Samson receives the grace accolade:

The Lord blessed him.

God's impatient Spirit was at work. Because God is disturbing.

The Lord blessed him and the Spirit of the Lord began to stir him.

The exact meaning of the word 'stirred' is uncertain – some say it means impelled, that Samson experienced divinely induced restlessness.

The Hebrew word that is translated 'stirred' is found in other biblical stories.

While Joseph languished in an Egyptian prison, Pharaoh's mind was 'troubled' by his dream and so he consulted the magicians and wise men of Egypt,[5] who couldn't help him. Pharaoh's turbulent state eventually led him to Joseph. Deliverance began with someone being agitated.

Another insomniac potentate, King Nebuchadnezzar[6] had restless nights too. His mind was churning, denying him sleep. Again, the proven sages of the day were summoned, but they were useless and couldn't speak clarity into his confusion. That led to Daniel being ushered onto the royal scene. Deliverance began with someone being agitated.

The psalmist tossed and turned too, as he thought about better days gone by and agonised over God's apparent absence:

I thought about the former days,

the years of long ago;

I remembered my songs in the night.

My heart mused and my spirit enquired:

'Will the LORD reject for ever?

Will he never show his favour again?

Has his unfailing love vanished forever?

Has his promise failed for all time?

Has God forgotten to be merciful?

Has he in anger withheld his compassion?'[7]

The word 'stirred' also speaks of waves of passion that come and go, like the crashing back and forth of a boiling tide, pounding the sand. The word speaks of a bell that is sometimes rung and then is silent; like a footstep that is heard and then is not ...

Another translator has it: 'the spirit of the Lord began to drive him hard'.[8] The words conjure up a picture of compulsion and then calm, the Spirit urging, but never settling upon him. Still another image created is that of a throbbing heartbeat, beating fast, as the Spirit stirs him, and then settling down again.

Until next time.

Just as Jesus was 'driven out' into the wilderness by the Spirit of God (the word Mark uses is most often used to describe demons being 'driven out', so 'sent' is a tame, benign translation), so something strange, turbulent and perhaps almost violent was happening within Samson.

Perhaps, when we think of the Spirit, we think of a dove – and for good reason. The Holy Spirit is often described as descending with whispering wings, gently, peacefully.

But sometimes the Spirit comes rushing to toss over the tables of our complacency, urging us, compelling us, distressing us and thrusting us quickly into a turbulent emotional wilderness.

The Spirit-agitated have caught a sense of what could be and what shouldn't be.

They have dreamed and perhaps their dreams have begun to crystallise into strategies and they actually believe that they can change the world.

They can:

Make poverty history.

Stop the effluent evil that is human trafficking.

Bring a smile of hope to the family next door that is being ripped apart by conflict.

Campaign for that abandoned waste ground to be
turned into a small park, an oasis in the barrenness of
the housing estate; build a play area in that place where
currently gangs linger and syringes are discarded ...

But it's only the agitated that will do this world-changing.

Agitation is the prelude to action. The world will never be
changed by those who are contented and complacent.

It's the angry, the irritated, the outraged, the frustrated,
the clumsily outspoken, the irritatingly persistent, the get-
under-your-skin naggers: these are the world-changers.

They wrestle, though, with many sleepless nights.
They hold a hundred conversations and dominate
most of them, so determined are they to get an
audience for what burns a hole in them.

They fret that no one really understands and at
times feel an unbearable loneliness, as if they are
lost in space, yet hemmed in by a crowd.

They feel like refugees when others feel quite at home.

They become monochrome and predictable. Sometimes
they rant and become unkind, or boring. *Change
the record, please. We've heard all this before.*

And, in their agitation, they live close to tears
much of the time. Others insist: don't worry.

*If only I could stop worrying, they say. I've
seen what I've seen and I can't unsee it.*

They know this truth and perhaps are haunted
by the realisation that they will carry the 'gift'
of agitation with them to the grave.

It will not leave them because they succeed in making a difference. Any breakthroughs, ironically, will make things worse, for they will redouble their efforts to bring change. In changing something, they will believe that they might just change everything. There will be no stopping now. At times they will despise their agitation.

But we need more agitated leaders. Agitated politicians. Agitated disciples. Agitating liturgy, which punches rather than placates us, which takes our breath away and throws down the gauntlet to our souls, daring us to join the revolution.

We need agitating preaching that creeps up on us when we're relaxed and smiling and bites us in the rear end. Teaching that assaults the mind and gets under the skin, so that, long after the service is over, we're still at work.

Cogitating.

Ruminating.

Strategising.

Groaning and interceding.

Samson was receiving a gift of agitation, from the God who really is disturbing.

—   —   —   —   —

The agitating work began in Samson's soul when he was in Mahaneh Dan - the camp of Dan. Remember that Samson was from the Danite tribe and they had been unsuccessful in securing their inheritance in the land distribution arrangement set out by Joshua. That meant that some of Samson's tribe apparently lived a semi-nomadic existence in the shadow of towns like Ekron.

Ekron. We talked about that city before. As Samson stared at its fortified walls, surely a ball of indignation filled his gut, his mouth tasting a bitter bile. *It should be our city, not theirs.*

God had promised the Hebrews that city, but it had never been successfully claimed. Instead of being settlers, some of their tribe lived like displaced nomads. Called to freedom, they lived under the heel of oppression instead.

The shame of it. As a tribe, Dan was considered to be of no account, living on the outskirts of Israel, like a 'horde of beggars on the doors of a rich man's house'.[9]

There was no doubt: the Spirit was unsettling him, provoking him. Would he respond, or do what many Spirit-agitated souls do and succumb instead to selfish hedonism?

\-   \-   \-   \-   \-

There are times when I just want a life.

I don't want a purpose-driven life.

There are times – seasons, even – when I'm not excited by purpose and I certainly don't want to be driven.

I just want a life. Benign survival. Soak-up-the-gravy-on-the-plate kind of pleasure.

Existence unsullied by concern, vision or expectation.

Just another day.

Just another day.

Sometimes, I want that life.

Samson did. He preferred what he could see, what he could touch, to what he might dream about or sacrifice for.

It was in the Valley of Sorek and the area of
the camp of Dan - here Samson saw agitating
sights that seared and stirred his soul.

But it was also here, in the Valley of
Sorek, that a certain lady lived.

Her name was Delilah. He would meet her years later.

Even if she was quite unaware of it, she was waiting,
waiting to tame the angry, agitated Samson.

She'd calm him down alright.

Waiting to satiate him with her caresses, to soothe his
furrowed brow with her gentle fingertips, waiting to
hand him over to blindness and torture and death.

He didn't know it and neither did she. But she was
waiting. Waiting for him to decide that he was entitled
to a little pleasure, a little happiness at last.

Meanwhile, the Spirit was giving him the once-over,
pulsing within him, stoking a growing rage, trying
to fashion the beginnings of a heart that just might
be open to this idea: everything can change.

-     -   -   -   -

It's an old Latvian folk song, often sung in church circles,
usually among children, although not exclusively:

> *If you're happy and you know it clap your hands.*
> *Stomp your feet. Say Amen.*

If you're happy and you know it
then your face should surely show it.
If you're happy and you know it clap your hands.

But here's an uncomfortable question:

Are Christians actually any happier because we are Christians? More importantly, are we supposed to be?

At first glance, I thought the answer should be yes.

Happiness is to know the Saviour

Living a life within His favour,

Having a change in my behaviour,

Happiness is the Lord.

The offer of happiness has often been part of the evangelistic sales pitch: get Jesus and get a happier, more contented, peaceful heart. Happiness is here. Come and get it. You'll feel great.

Happiness is a new creation,

Jesus and me in close relation,

Having a part in His salvation,

Happiness is the Lord.

And the Christian message *is* called *the gospel.* That means 'good news', doesn't it?

Doesn't the Bible say that the fruit of the Spirit includes some joy?

Real joy is mine, no matter if teardrops start;

I've found the secret, it's Jesus in my heart!

Happiness is to be forgiven,

Living a life that's worth the living,

Taking a trip that leads to Heaven,

Happiness is the Lord! [10]

So aren't we supposed to be happier than everyone else? I think the answer is yes – and no.

If even pondering the question is awkward, know that our pondering this is vital – lest we offer something that we can't deliver. These days, happiness is the elusive holy grail; everyone is frantically hunting for it. Carlin Flora, writing on the *Psychology Today* website, points to the desperate pursuit of happiness:

> *Welcome to the happiness frenzy, now peaking at a Barnes & Noble near you: in 2008 4,000 books were published on happiness, while a mere 50 books on the topic were released in 2000. The most popular class at Harvard University is about positive psychology and at least 100 other universities offer similar courses. Happiness workshops for the post-collegiate set abound and each day 'life coaches' promising bliss to potential clients hang out their shingles.* [11]

If surveys are to be believed, then Christians are more likely to be happy. More Christians describe themselves as 'very happy' than Americans as a whole, according to a Pew Research Centre survey that was recently conducted in the USA. [12] Almost half – 43 per cent – of evangelical Protestants described themselves as happy, compared to only 34 per cent of Americans.

And perhaps they profess to be happier for good reason: that's why I answer tentatively in the affirmative. Christian Smith, a sociologist at the University of North Carolina, said there are many possible reasons why evangelical Protestants rate higher than others on happiness surveys:

> *Religion, especially Christianity, emphasises forgiveness, reduction of anxiety through prayer, gratitude and other virtues. In addition to this, evangelical churches provide various tools, teachings, beliefs and practices that tend to increase happiness.*[13]

That makes sense.

But I still have other cautions. It's still yes and no.

Of course Christians may be happier because they embrace a lifestyle that is not just Christian, but is being lived according to the Maker's directions.

That said, I think we need to be wary of Christianity where personal happiness is guaranteed; and I don't say this just because I meet so many Christians who are battling depression.

First off, that survey.

We have to face the uncomfortable fact that a lot of us Christians don't tell the truth. So when we're asked if we're happy we insist that we are, because we think that we're supposed to be. We see happiness as a sign of authentic Christianity and so, in wanting to be in, we profess to be so.

Ruth Tucker, a missions professor at Calvin Theological Seminary, wrote about happiness in her recent book *Walking Away from Faith*.[14] The Pew poll, she says, simply shows that Christians are expected to be happy. And she even quoted that song:

We all know the song 'If You're Happy and You Know It.' There are a number of little jingles like that about happiness in children's choruses. Happiness is kind of a mark for an evangelical. We make it important in our choruses, in our megachurches and in evangelism.

Tucker said she doesn't think happiness is necessarily biblical, but it is preached from church pulpits as a Christian calling.

So perhaps we tick yes to the happiness question because we feel our response is dutiful.

However, more importantly, Jesus didn't offer happiness as an assured benefit to His would-be followers. For just about every one of His close inner circle, discipleship meant hardship, tears and martyrdom. Elderly John was an exception – although he spent some of his twilight years in exile on Patmos, which was hardly Pleasantville.

The contemporary Church's pursuit of happiness is markedly different from those who engaged in Christianity historically:

Christians in the Early Church did not expect to have happiness before death. Much of Augustine's City of God *criticises those who seek perfect happiness in this world. Original sin, Augustine wrote, made earthly happiness impossible. It's only relatively recently, since the 18th century, that people expected religion to make them happy. In a way, it's a perverse affirmation of the Enlightenment.*[15]

Those who decided to follow Jesus welcomed the stunning news of the kingdom, where life could be done as God intended, where sin could be freely forgiven and where peace with God was offered through the finished work of Christ.

But they also embraced the real possibility of being beaten, hated, martyred, burned out and burned up. They embraced the responsibilities of prayer, the challenge to live provocatively, the call to love their enemies and the command to embrace the leper. They had said yes to an invitation to die to self, turn the other cheek, give extravagantly and serve without applause or recognition. They were now to be the people who would not scurry for the top tables that are usually allocated to the VIPs, but would be more delighted to wash the sweaty, dusty feet of the arriving guests. No longer living to just fritter away their days on the altars of their own pleasure, they made the choice to live for something bigger, better and greater. The kingdom of God.

But the promise of that kingdom did *not* guarantee that they would be happier.

They would have joy: that mingling of hope and peace that irrationally sustains us when circumstances try to insist that we have no right to feel positive. Think of Paul and Silas singing hymns at midnight, the wounds from their beating still stark and deep. Broken, but joyful.

But nobody ever promised that they would grin more: for they would be the blessedly agitated, driven hard by the same Spirit that drove Samson.

Perhaps Samson didn't reach his full potential because, through foolhardy recklessness, purchased sex and high-stakes gambling, he constantly stomped around, relentless in the pursuit of happiness, rather than giving himself to the purposeful, agitating pull of the Spirit.

The agitated are indeed blessed. But not always happy with it.

Seven:
WHAT YOU SEE IS WHAT GETS YOU

'Samson followed his eyes, which is why the Philistines gouged them out.' – The Talmud[1]

It's what anyone who has ever worked in youth ministry (and youth camps in particular) knows only too well.

It's rather obvious that teenage years are complicated by raging hormones and turbulent emotions. No news there.

But what might be less understood is this: the vulnerable time in any youth camp is the night when there's a sense that God is powerfully at work.

Emotions are stirred.

People go forward to respond and ask for prayer at the end of the service.

Earnest pledges are made to God.

Tears of repentance flow freely.

And then the service finally draws to a close.

Quick. Bring out the torches (flashlights, for any American friends).

Send out the patrols.

Scour the bushes.

Because tonight's the night when you're more likely to stumble over couples who are doing a little more than praying together. Perhaps we might be a little shocked at this news? What happened back in the service? Wasn't that a call to renewed commitment and holiness? Didn't all that mean something? Was it all just a religious game?

Yes, it meant a lot. The pledges were sincere. But when we're stirred, we're stirred. We are not segmented creatures, sectioned neatly into the spiritual, the emotional, the physical and the sexual.

It's all part of the one same deal. Us.

So when we're stirred by the Spirit, and when we open ourselves up and become vulnerable, we're in the zone where we're likely to be stirred up emotionally – and sexually – too.

Look again at Samson's unfolding story – but this time, delete the chapter break. (Even the chapter breaks in the Old Testament were placed there only 550 years ago.[2] They're relatively new.)

> *The Spirit of the LORD began to stir him*
> *... and he went down to Timnah and saw*
> *there a young Philistine woman ...*

Let me spell it out.

He was stirred by the Spirit.
And he saw a woman.

Okay, time for another health warning. Brace yourself – because the Bible talks about the erotic in a way that we usually don't ...

-      -   -   -   -

I hadn't been very explicit during my sermon on Samson. I simply said that his story was charged with eroticism. But that was enough to light the blue touch paper. The man jumped up, yelled 'This is a disgrace!' and stormed out of the church service, obviously convinced that any reference to sex was out of order (but that disruptive and rude behaviour was entirely okay).

Why did he react in that way?

Perhaps it's a big fat Greek hangover that made him (and some of us) so reluctant to talk about sex, especially in a church context. The Greek philosophical notion that the physical is inherently evil spilled over into the Church in the earliest days, making 'spiritual' conversation kosher but discussion about anything as earthy as sex off limits.

For whatever reason, straight talk about sex ignites reaction in the Church. A Baptist minister friend got into hot water for talking about sex in the pulpit.

Well, not sex *in the pulpit*.

Sex during a sermon.

No ...

You know what I mean.

Whatever the reasons for our inhibitions and our tendency to titter and whisper about sex, the writers of Scripture certainly didn't share our hesitation.

If you own a Bible, you have a highly explicit book in your home. Not convinced?

The imagery of eating is sometimes used in the Old Testament to describe oral sex. That's why Proverbs phrases a reference to a philandering woman:

> *This is the way of an adulteress: She eats and wipes her mouth and says, 'I've done nothing wrong.'*[3]

I know. It's graphic.

Honey is used as a highly erotic symbol in the Song of Solomon.[4]

I've already said Samson's story is filled with eroticism. Bill Clinton and Samson share something in common. Monica Lewinsky revealed specific anatomical details about the presidential appendage, but Mr Clinton was not the first public figure to have such personal intimacies unveiled to the world. The rabbis insisted that Samson's size mattered, declaring in The Talmud that God 'blessed' him, using a word, *b'amato*, which is a euphemism for penis.[5] It also means 'cubit' – which is 18 inches. They even said that he was endowed 'just like other men'. Worrying.

Of course, those rabbis loved to exaggerate – they also taught that Samson was able to lift two mountains at a time. That's a relief ...

Forgive the bluntness, but the ancients also speculated about Samson's ability to produce semen, insisting that his seed was 'like a fast-flowing stream'.[6]

His story has a peppering of bawdy wedding-night humour. A prostitute's seedy boudoir. And some sex that involves people being tied up.

I know. Perhaps you've been taught that Delilah tying Samson up in knots was part of some elaborate Near-Eastern game. I think that bondage sex is the more likely explanation.

But all this lurid stuff presents a danger to us.

Like a flashing red neon sign that draws the eye, we can focus on Samson's badness and be oblivious to any goodness. When that happens, we just write him off, sentence passed. He was a brainless, immoral man and that's that. Case closed. Samson, an idiotic fool of whom the old joke is surely true:

God created Adam and informed him that He had given him a brain and a penis. The brain was a good gift as it allowed him to do many things. The penis was also a good thing as it allowed the race to continue. The problem was that Adam's limited blood supply meant that he could only use one of them at a time.[7]

And the riddle that Samson would share at his wedding probably started out as a bawdy comment shared with leering men who were joking about the wedding night to come. Although the riddle was obviously related to his exploits with the lion, it carries strong erotic overtones as well.

Honey.

Eaters.

And then, when things went very wrong at his wedding reception, Samson uses a sexual euphemism to accuse his new-found 'friends': 'If you had not ploughed with my heifer, you would not have solved my riddle.'

Look past the uncomfortable reality that he has just referred to his bride as a cow and notice the imagery of ploughing, yet another sexual innuendo.

So we are about to go into uncomfortable territory.

This blessed and stirred man didn't realise what we all need to know.

The eyes have it. It's not that what we see is what we get. Rather, what we see is what gets us.

— — — — —

It's like the ominous tolling of a funeral bell, the sombre sound signalling foreboding. And we've only just got introduced to the young adult that was Samson.

> *Samson went down to Timnah and saw*
> *there a young Philistine woman.*

Went down.

The imagery is deliberate: Samson is starting his long descent already. Samson 'goes down' to Timnah three times and he also goes down to Ashkelon and to Etam. At the end of his life, after his capture, Samson will be 'made to go down' to Gaza. His topological descents mirror his moral decline.

We are not told her name, this alluring Philistine girl, but she was the first of three Philistine women (Delilah was probably a Philistine, although we're not specifically told so). Foreign women had a special allure for Hebrew men – reputed to be more sexually permissive and mysterious than Hebrew women, they had the mystique of the unfamiliar, the unexplored.

It's the oldest trick in the book.

The grass is greener.

> *Samson went down to Timnah and saw*
> *there a young Philistine woman.*

He told his parents that he had seen the woman and that he wanted what he saw.

It all starts with the eyes. And not only does
the writer of Samson's story want us to know
that disaster begins with what we see.

In the beginning, Eve saw.

> When the woman saw that the fruit of the tree was
> good for food and pleasing to the eye, and also desirable
> for gaining wisdom, she took some and ate it.[8]

Samson has been stirred within by the Spirit, but, instead of
responding to that divine impulsion in his heart, he goes after
a very tangible compulsion – that which he saw with his eyes.

Flesh.

For Israel at that time, the eyes had it. This was a period
in their history when instead of doing what was right
in God's eyes, they did what was right (*yashar*) in their
eyes.[9] The same word is used of Samson here: as he
insists, 'she's right for me', *yashar* is the word used.

Instead of the strange guy in town, Samson is
already becoming just like everybody else.

What his eyes see dominates him.

And the sight of the woman cancels
out his own common sense.

-    -   -   -   -

It's as if he knows full well that what he is doing is insane, but he doesn't care.

The term used in the text to describe Samson's anticipated Timnite bride is the common term 'woman' (*'ishah*) and not the more acceptable term 'maiden' (*na'arah*), which is used to refer to a chaste young woman. Samson calls his wife righteous and then uses a term which implies that she was nothing of the sort.

It's as if he is saying, 'This poison is right for me' ...

And, of course, the eyes, once focused, block the ears to sound advice.

He refuses to listen to his parents.

Like an overgrown petulant kid who, with trembling lip, threatens to scream the toy shop down if he doesn't get what he wants, so Samson stamps his feet, bunches his fists and stands his ground. And the conversation that had begun with Samson addressing both his father and his mother now narrows to his father only. Perhaps Samson knew that battling his strong-willed, confident, even manipulative mother would be a waste of time. His father would buckle and succumb with such little effort, an easy conquest.

-        -   -   -   -

If being stirred spiritually and emotionally truly opens us up sexually, then this stark sentence is a fact and needs to be slapped onto every church like a government health warning:

Churches are the perfect environment to nurture immorality.

We talk intimately. We laugh together, cry together. We hug and hold each other and say that we love each other.

That's why when Paul wrote to young Timothy about the way the sexes should treat each other respectfully and carefully, he was being prudent, not prudish.

'Treat younger men as brothers, older women as mothers, and younger women as sisters, with absolute purity.'[10]

He is reminding us to be diligent and attentive as we share our lives together. Life must be approached with our eyes wide open, not in the sleepiness of emotional cruise control.

He calls us to realise that *we* are entirely capable of immorality. Us. Me. You.

Some of us think we would never stoop to such behaviour. *We should watch when we stand, lest we fall.*

We think we are above such temptations. *But the reason we have not failed in that area is not because of moral superiority, but lack of opportunity so far. No one has ever made an offer. Only if they did, would we discover how we'd actually respond.*

Some of us share about our marriages and sex lives with trusted friends. But we even need to take care in those contexts. In the name of openness and accountability, we can end up 'sharing' to the point that it becomes voyeuristic; where the private intimacy of the bedroom is violated and our frank conversations unhealthily stir imagination and fantasy in those with whom we 'share'.

And then, in church, we connect so innocently. I think most affairs between Christians begin with avid discussions about the Bible and deepen through shared times of prayer. Sex comes much later. Holier connections have been long cemented before anything physical takes place.

I'm not suggesting that we walk around in abject terror, fearing every member of the opposite sex as a potential ruiner of our souls. Some men make women feel that they are being treated suspiciously, as wanton sirens who are just waiting to ensnare them.

I'm just suggesting that we are radical and clear about what we focus on and who we dream about.

If your eye offends you, said Jesus, gouge it out.

If your hand offends, cut it off.

Jesus obviously meant this metaphorically. That's worth saying, because Origen, an Early Church father, took Jesus' words literally and castrated himself, only to discover that he had misunderstood that text. That would mess up your week ...

But Jesus *was* calling us to a radical, absolutely decisive approach.

Do we have people who can confront us, to whom we have given permission to believe not the best about us, but the worst about us? Or will we deflect awkward challenges by acting offended and outraged?

We must allow others to believe the *worst* about us, because we are capable of the worst.

After all, you and I are related to Samson, as fellow members of the human race. We're sons and daughters of Adam.

That's us.

All of us.

The Adam's Family.

- - - - -

Samson's problem started with his eyes.

He saw a Philistine woman.

Later, the writer of his story will tell us that he saw a prostitute.

His eyes got him again. And the fateful day would soon come when his eyes would fall upon another woman, by the name of Delilah. There would be a tragic irony in his story, because there comes a moment when, at last, he gets a clearer vision of who God is and he prays a prayer that comes closest to intimacy and urgency with the Lord. At last he sees.

But that happens after the Philistines have successfully arrested him and put him to work as a slave.

Having first gouged out his eyes.

Eight:
JESUS WORKS AT A RUBBISH DUMP

'God ... specialises in working in the
midst of a mess.' – George Verwer[1]

He's always so cheerful, that's the strange
and slightly wonderful thing.

He sits in his little booth at the entrance to the rubbish dump.
In the winter months, he huddles around a single-bar electric
heater. I drive up, he slides his window open and he says, 'Hey,
how are you?', his breath billowing a cloud in the cold, his
smile somehow bringing a little thaw to the chill of the day.

I tell him what I always tell him.

Two sacks of domestic rubbish. Thanks.

He nods and smiles again. But I don't think that
this is the job of his dreams; that when he was at
school he confessed to a strange ambition: *I'd like
to work as an attendant at a rubbish dump.*

But every time I stop by, eager to get rid of my
fetid black bin bags, bulging with trash, he acts
as if I am delivering priceless treasure.

I just want to hurl my swollen bags into the
giant dumpster and get out of there fast.

It's the stench I hate.

It's sour.

Rotten. A whiff of fermenting decay lingers over the
dump like a thick cloud: you can almost taste it.

And I can't stand the sense of chaos. Seagulls scurry over
untamed heaps, flitting here and there like junior-sized
vultures, beady eyes looking for decomposing snacks.
Every now and again something spooks them and they rise
as one above the putrid piles, only to swoop down once
more to continue their picking. Men driving bulldozers
shove great stacks of garbage into unmarked graves,
landfill that will burp methane for decades to come.

I don't know the name of the smiling rubbish dump sentry.

I'm grateful that he seems to like his work.

Unlike that anonymous smiling man who sits in his booth,
God doesn't wear a fluorescent yellow jacket, or a hard hat.
But He is very much at work in the disarray, in the mess
and sometimes in the midst of the filth that is in us.

Sound a little extreme, this use of the
word *filth*? I use it thoughtfully.

No matter how changed we are, how deliberate our
behaviour, how seemingly ordered our private world,
how pristine our purity, compared to the holiness of God,
we smell very bad. Our scent is the stench of death.

Isaiah[2] declares that our righteousness is as filthy rags.
Brace yourself, for here comes yet more bluntness.

The phrase 'filthy rags' has been softened in the
translation because of our sensibilities. It literally means
'our righteousness is like soiled menstrual clothes'.

Yuk.

But perhaps, although the phrase is crude
and graphic, it's painfully true.

Our lives are a jumble of grubby motives, aspirations smeared
by selfishness and nose-wrinkling habits. We spew words
that stain others' hearts and lives. We allow our minds to
meander into fantasies that should make our souls blush.

Yet, because of grace, He works in us.

He works, wading through the mush and the junk, squelching through the stagnant slurry of our sins.

God works at the rubbish dump of me.

You.

And Samson.

-　　　-　　　-　　　-　　　-

Let's face it. It's awkward, to say the least.

Samson was being led by his eyes and his loins,
into a marriage with a Philistine woman.

Sleeping with the enemy.

He was supposed to be leading his people to war against
them, not becoming one of their in-laws. But look at him, as he
insists, absolutely, that his parents get that woman as his bride.

His jaw is fixed. He stares his father down. He shows no
respect for his parents, no concern about his Nazirite calling,
no loyalty to his own people and no clarity in his ethics.

He is a stubborn brute.

But not only is this an ugly picture, there's also an awkward theological conundrum in the episode.

God is stirring, impelling, driving Samson hard.

Samson's proposed marriage to a Philistine woman was clearly prohibited under the law.[3]

Samson knew that. His parents knew that too, although their concerns might have been more about Samson breaking cultural expectations rather than his disobedience to the prohibitions of the law.

But here's the problem.

God was involved in this plan, which clearly violated what God Himself had previously said.

God seems to be breaking His own rules. Flouting His own laws.

Look at it. There's no attempt by the narrator to excuse God, to cover for Him:

> *His parents did not know that this was from the LORD, who was seeking an occasion to confront the Philistines; for at that time they were ruling over Israel.*[4]

What's going on? Is God not trustworthy? Does He ignore His own principles? If that's true, then anyone could insist that God was leading them to clearly disobey a specific biblical command, on the basis that God Himself was overriding it.

But because God *uses* a circumstance doesn't make Him the architect of that circumstance.

There's no record that God commanded Samson to marry a Philistine.

But God was using Samson's headstrong attitude, and
his pulsating hormones, to get His will done.

God works on rubbish dumps. He is able to sift through the scraps and the junk of our foolishness and turn those moments of madness into treasure.

God is the redeemer. He turns around what was
meant for evil and makes it into something good.

He can turn our mistakes into milestones.

Consider Israel's insane decision to demand a human king.
They rejected the God who had rescued them from the slavery
of Egypt. They turned their back on the One who had patiently
borne with their whining and idolatry in the wilderness.

*No, we want a king, so we can be like everybody
else.* There's that herd mentality again.

And so they got Saul. Bad decision. Bad king.
Terrible, in fact. It all ended in tears.

But then God dives head first into the midst of
their mad choice and redeems the situation.

You want a human king, still? He gives them David and Solomon.
Israel's worst decision births a golden era. Peace, economic
growth, good, godly leadership. A terrible choice redeemed.

But it doesn't stop there. Out of that house of
kings comes Jesus. That beautiful life was birthed
from a royal line that began with rebellion.

Did God want Israel to reject Him? *No.*

Did God turn that decision around and use that
royal lineage to bring Jesus to us? *Yes.*

But the redeemer hadn't finished yet.

Jesus was marched to the cross, the victim of a kangaroo
court, the work of some demonically religious cheerleaders
who whipped a crowd into a frenzy. Yet another herd, this one
eager for blood. He died at the hands of the brutal Romans.

Is God for injustice, for religious hypocrisy, for mob rule? *No.*

But God turned that around. Once again, He waded
through the simmering, putrid mounds of human
history and got His will done in the midst of it all.

Christ died for our sins. The ultimate turnaround, the most
stunning redemption act: atrocious human behaviour, turned
around to serve the purposes of divine love and grace.

He's the turnaround God. That doesn't give us a licence to
blunder on in the madness of rebellion, just so that we can give
God an opportunity to reverse the effects of our foolishness.

It just means that we need to remember
that God works on rubbish dumps.

What's this got to do with Samson?

God was active in the mess again, knee-
deep in the muck of Samson's lust.

He works in the mess of our sin. And He works
in the mess of ridiculous religion too.

-      -   -   -   -

The television evangelist was working up quite a sweat now and so was I. Watching and listening was agony. Depressingly, he was preaching utter drivel, twisting one scripture after another, building his case with biblical quotations that were wrenched violently out of context. Even more depressingly, the congregation was lapping it up. They were eager for more, and no wonder.

He was painting a picture of a spiritual Disneyland for their delight.

'It is not God's will that any Christian suffer', the white-suited man insisted. That's interesting, considering the blood-soaked document that is the New Testament.

'Everyone should be healed and, if they're not, then it could be because of sin ...'

Thanks a lot. Now I feel ill and guilty with it. And what of those dear, faithful saints sitting over there in the section reserved for people who use wheelchairs? They navigate their way through life with stoic bravery: are they now to be collectively shamed by the preacher man who skips around, Bible in hand?

It gets worse. He thunders that my sickness might be a result of a sinful act that my great-great-great-grandfather did.

Great. I'll dig him up and slap him.

And still worse. I need to send a large offering to the evangelist, 'beyond what I can naturally do, because it needs to be an act of faith' and he'll take authority over my life.

Oh, that's handy. I can charge it to my Visa card. 'All will be well', he promises. 'You can't outgive God', he insists.

Wow. This is the old system of indulgences, dressed up as faith.

This guy is a thousand miles off beam.

Yes, he is.

And, irritatingly, people *do* get healed through his ministry.

Believe me, I'd like to prove that they don't. And obviously sometimes miracles are claimed that are not miracles at all.

That said, I'm convinced that there are genuine, God-given miracles that take place, even as the telephone number comes up on the screen and the Visa symbol appears.

Because God works on rubbish dumps.

We tend towards simplistic thinking – that people and ministries and books and churches are either right or they're wrong. But nobody is totally right about everything. Nobody is totally wrong about everything either.

And God's involvement in our lives doesn't imply His endorsement.

Because people are healed doesn't mean that God is pleased with the Visa/healing shenanigans. On the contrary, His nose wrinkles. Perhaps it all makes Him gag.

But He's good at being the redeemer.

So God blesses ministers who are tin-pot dictators and who bully their congregations into submission. He works through the proud, the aggressively ambitious and the vain.

He genuinely works through leaders who preach angelically on Sundays and then live immorally on Mondays.

I'll say it again, just in case. None of this gives us an excuse to live carelessly, presumptuously insisting that God straighten out our messes. But surely we find encouragement and relief in knowing that God does not use only perfect people for His purposes. If that were true, He'd get nothing done.

And so He keeps turning things around.

And working on the rubbish dumps that are us.

Nine:
SECRET HONEY WILL MAKE US SICK

'We are so accustomed to disguise ourselves to others that in the end we become disguised to ourselves.' - François Duc de La Rochefoucauld[1]

Epic battles and, more specifically, epic victories, are meant to be shared.

The footballer skips and weaves his way through the defence and, with just seconds to go before the final whistle, drives the ball with a thunderous volley into the heart of the goal, billowing the net with a beautiful *thunk*. He looks up expectantly at the crowd, his arms aloft, his fist bunched in a punch of triumph. The crowd do their job: they yell and jump and high-five and, on the pitch, his teammates pile on him, jubilantly celebrating his brilliance.

The soldier comes home, bloodied and wearied from war, but the time comes for him and his proud family to gather at the palace. At last, he spends a minute or two whispering with the Queen. She asks him about the worst and best day of his life, when his courage won the day and he shone. She pins a medal for valour to his proud chest. His victory is shared, celebrated.

But sometimes fierce, terrible battles are fought and bloody skirmishes continue behind the veneer of a quiet smile. We carry ourselves with practised poise and we fix our smiles so that most people who meet us will never know that, just beneath the surface of our thin skin, a fight to the death rages. We hope that those we meet will not be too perceptive and catch a hint of distant gunfire, or any other sense that, within us, the terrible wrestling is ongoing.

Behind the closed door of our eyelids, lions bare their teeth and let out a throaty, deep roar that threatens to stop our hearts. And as we smile once more and chatter away about the weather, just inside us the lion crouches down, tendons taut, claws bared, ready and waiting to leap and tear our throats out.

-     -   -   -   -

It was the first time that Samson had felt the surge of power. How did it feel, when the Spirit of God rushed upon him? An urgent surge, a terrifying bolt, an electrifying flow? What he must have known was this – the enabling came from outside of himself. Suddenly, the stories, the confusing stirring, the impotent rage, as if something, someone, was calling him, urging him into action, started to make some sense. Perhaps he knew what this meant: the strength to kill lions signalled a strength to kill Philistines. And he was on his way to take unto himself a Philistine bride. And so perhaps he didn't want to know what he knew. It would be his secret. He'd keep it quiet, even from his parents. Especially from his mother. The narrator wants to make it very obvious to us: he didn't tell his parents about the lion – or about the honey that he would find later.

He kills the lion with ease. Purists argue that he has already broken his Nazirite vow, because he ended up touching a dead body (it's what happens when you kill something …).

What else was he supposed to do? And the Spirit of the Lord *did* come upon him to help him successfully fight off the attacking big cat.

But it's what happens later that presents a
problem, at least for an avowed Nazirite.

When we wrestle with lions in secret, things are only going to get worse.

Some time later, he revisits the carcass, perhaps to look, to
remember the moment of that most weird empowering.
But he goes beyond looking and scoops honey out of
the dried shell – blatantly disregarding his Nazirite vow
at this point. And then he draws others unwittingly into
his carelessness, giving some of the honey to his hapless
parents (which would have made them ritually unclean)
and, once again, not telling them where it had come from.

Although he was not to know it, this 'innocent' eating of
honey was the action that set off a series of other events
that would ultimately lead to the failure of his marriage
and then the arson murder of his wife and her family.
What began as a small, dark secret had terrible effects.

- - - - -

There's something about the way all this happens
that gives the impression of carelessness. It's like
Samson is ambling around, meandering, probing,
playing and creating more secrets as he does.

Samson plays a lot. It's not enough for him to notice the honey
and raise an eyebrow at the unusual sight. He has to eat some
and then he has to share some with his parents, as if he wants
for once to have that mother of his not in control, not knowing,
not being the one who met the angel, not being so certain.

But he's playing a dangerous game. Warriors and deliverers need to be wide awake, utterly alert, ready for action. Perhaps that's why God allowed the lion to strike, to shatter in a second Samson's oafish ambling. We need to be awake, for the lion is close. How many steps do you have to take towards uncleanness? Just a few. Everything is wrecked in a moment, or with a few taps on a computer keyboard. Just turn aside, take a look, no one will know, you deserve this ...

–   –   –   –   –

Without overworking it, we can't ignore the image of a roaring lion in Samson's story. It's interesting that we're told that Satan is just like that creature. Hungry. Circling.

I confess, sometimes I don't get the whole Satan trip. I want to dismiss him as the mythical bad guy in the comic book. I want to discard the horns and pitchfork-carrying character for good and insist that he just represents the power of evil.

But I can't do that. Jesus gives Satan the attribute of personhood and reveals him as a cunning strategist waiting to strike, ready to pounce. To Peter, the warning was grave: 'Satan has asked to sift you as wheat. But I have prayed for you, Simon, that your faith may not fail.'[2]

Vague, impersonal evil has no power of strategy, no personality or cunning. Much as I'd love to relegate Satan to being little more than a metaphor, I'm sorry to report that we too have a roaring lion after us. He's hungry. Intimidating.

One way to combat the wiles of Satan is to make sure that we avoid secrets. But that isn't as easy as it sounds.

Accountability groups have become quite fashionable. And they're certainly biblical. God wants us to find circles of friendship where we can confess our sins, face up to our faults and find supportive advice and prayer. But, in reality, letting others know about our inward battles isn't that easy. For one thing, we risk people disliking us if they find out the real truth about us. Then there's the issue of trust: are we really safe in revealing our true selves? And then the madness of temptation can mean that we feel so driven, so passionate about what we know is wrong but just feels so right, that we end up deceiving ourselves and sincerely believing that what is blatantly wrong might be justifiable. Hot desire cancels out cold logic.

Perhaps Samson would have done so much better as a man with a secret strength if he hadn't become a man who kept so many secrets.

‑ ‑ ‑ ‑ ‑

Before we leave the strange sight of the bees' nest found in the dried carcass of the lion, it's worth lingering just a moment longer. The carcass symbolised Samson passing his first big test. Confronted with the terrorising strength of the attacking lion, he finds greater strength in God, as the Spirit rushes upon him. Perhaps he is being nudged to realise that he really does have what it takes to be a warrior. So, now what, Samson? Will you just carry on with life and settle down with your Philistine wife?

But the passing of the first test provides an opportunity for a second moment of temptation. His pilgrimage back to the lion's carcass leads him to discover the honey that now nestled within it.

The honey was only there because God gave him power.

The honey was there because Samson had won his first tussle.

The honey was, in a sense, the fruit of God's smile.

But he wasn't supposed to touch it, as we've seen.
That would violate his vow. And he did.

Sometimes the blessing of God brings honey. That's
certainly true in Christian leadership. Success means
that people like you. You discover the sweetness of
being popular, sought after. People recognise your name.
They covet your advice. They like to be around you.

And you know that the honey is only there
because of God's kindness in the first place.

But that's when the real test begins. Will success destroy you?

Will you act like someone who thinks they're special and demand special treatment?

Will you start to think that you are not like others and
start to play fast and loose with your morals, because you
think that a silver spoon of grace is in your mouth?

Honey is sweet. But it can also be sweet-tasting poison.

Ten:
FRIENDSHIP IS AN ART

'Friendship is unnecessary, like
philosophy, like art ... It has no survival
value; rather it is one of those things that
give value to survival.' – C.S. Lewis[1]

The wedding day is usually long hoped for, much
mused about and extremely costly. It's supposed
to be one of the happiest days of one's life.

Magical. Romantic. Delightful. The easy laughter of
friends. The veteran connection of family. The coming
together for one purpose – to celebrate with two
people who are in love and to wish them well.

Surely Samson hoped the day would be a great day.

But it didn't turn out that way: on the contrary. An extravagant,
expensive seven-day party ended with rage, death and
tears. It's a drinking party at that – as we've seen, unusual
for a man who has taken a Nazirite vow. Once again his
vows are tossed aside without too much thought ...

But at the end of a week of jubilation, the bride and groom
were not waved off to begin their happy lives together.
Instead, a tearful bride is distraught. And a furious
bridegroom stomps off to embark on a killing spree.

It was his wedding day, or, more accurately, his
wedding week. And it was a disaster. The events that

unfolded that week would ultimately lead to his wife's death. So how can we mess up our better days?

—   —   —   —   —

It sounds like rent-a-friend and, in a way, it was. Samson took no friends of his own to his wedding – an ominous fact. How sad it is that Samson had no true friends to be at his side on his day of days, his wedding. And so the Philistines enlist thirty 'companions', thirty carefully selected men to stand at his side.

Forget that dreamy notion of hospitable Philistines being kind to the sad loner from Israel. The word used to describe them is anything but friendly. In fact the word 'sin' is found buried in the Hebrew term that describes these companions. They are minders. Sentries. Spies. Look at what prompted the sudden conscription of 'these friends' – it was when the Philistines *saw* Samson.

This was a posse of burly low-lifes who were forcibly conscripted to keep a wary eye on Samson. The Philistines knew that he was a Hebrew and therefore an enemy. A gang of thirty should have been sufficient to keep him under control – and military units in those days often came in thirties. Those that stood with him had never met him before and were only there to control him, to make sure that he behaved himself, to tame the potentially volatile bridegroom. He was friendless.

As are most.

True friendship is rare. The art of friendship isn't taught in school: the mistaken assumption is that we will know how to 'do' friendship. But generally, we don't. Old reruns of *Friends* remain popular: we all yearn for what that laughing gaggle of pals have.

At the risk of resorting to stereotypes, I've observed that women are generally better at prioritising time for friendship, and then opening up about what's going on in their private worlds. But when we don't make time (and in our breathless world it will usually demand great effort) or move deeper than superficial small talk, then we miss out on one of the greatest joys of life: a life shared. But Samson went friendless to his own wedding feast. A useful question might be to ask: why?

\-   \-   \-   \-   \-

If you want to be alone, then be a know-it-all.

Samson loved, maybe even craved, being in the know. The presenting of a riddle, a usual form of entertainment at a Near-Eastern wedding, seems innocent enough. But it was a riddle that was impossible to crack; only someone who had been with Samson in the vineyard of Timnah would have been able to decode it. He would have been able to wander around the party, the literal know-it-all, and smirk at them as they stood frustrated and marooned in their confusion. He knew there was no way they could crack the code.

Unless they attacked his bride, he was invincible, secure in his castle of knowledge.

Watch him hold out – for seven days. He watches his thirty Philistine 'friends' get increasingly frustrated. And then, desperate to know the answer and win the bet, they start to gang up on his wife. She applies pressure: she 'lures' him – the same word that is used of Delilah: the enemy of our souls is cunning, but not creative.

Now, his bride is distraught – and all over the silly game and a trivial bet. Surely Samson will bring the madness to an end. It was just foolish. But the immature never know when to stop playing, don't realise that there comes a moment to call time on the game and start acting like sensible adults again. He loves to hold the secret, to know the answer that no one else knows.

I wonder why. Does the man who sets uncrackable riddles want them to know that he, too, is an unfathomable riddle, one that he himself can't decode or begin to understand? Or does he just want to gain the upper hand?

I've seen this scenario repeatedly in a Christian context. A thirst to be knowledgeable, to be seen as spiritually deeper, can hijack any of us. Pride coils itself around a genuine hunger to know God more intimately and, before long, we consider that we are guardians of 'secrets' that nobody else possesses. The Early Church had a big problem with a 'knowledge cult' – Gnosticism. Insisting that they had been given secret wisdom that no one else possessed, the Gnostics threatened to tear the Church apart. People who have decided that their faith is deeper than everyone else's are highly dangerous. And when they get their sticky hands onto a leadership position, they are even more dangerous.

Samson is unyielding and completely insensitive to the concerns and frailties of others. Instead of wanting to please his bride at her wedding feast, he is apparently unmoved by her trauma. Instead, he makes a pious speech that makes it appear that he is very close to his parents, when in fact that was not the case at all. He turns his secretive behaviour – in not telling his parents about the honey and the carcass – into something almost noble.

In the end, we see that you can win an argument and lose a spouse. He wins the riddle, but, at the end of the feast, his wife is given to someone else. He's triumphant and, at that moment, a total loser with it.

—   —   —   —   —

But before disaster struck, he told her.

He told her what he had told no one else.

He told her what he had carefully kept concealed from his parents.

He bared his soul and shared his strange story.

And perhaps he didn't just tell her that he found honey in the carcass of a lion, but told her about the crouching predator in the vineyard and about the power that had rushed upon him and the alien feeling that the empowering gave him. Perhaps he also told her how he tore the lion apart with ease, surprising himself as he did, stunned by the sudden power of his own hands ....

He opened up.

For the first time, the man who had no friends of his own at his wedding, the man who kept a great distance between himself and his parents, showed himself.

As we saw earlier, our greatest need is to be known. Now, even in his headstrong arrogance, Samson at last opens himself to someone else, taking the risk, going into emotional territory that was probably terrifying for him.

And what does she do?

She betrays him.

Perhaps he always knew that she would: she had said nothing about wanting to pass the secret on, to enable her own countrymen to win the sick bet: but she did.

And so Samson ignited in a fury that came from that betrayal. The one time he lays his soul bare, his trust is trashed. Enraged, he goes on a terrible killing spree and pays the lost bet with the clothes stolen from the corpses of those he murders.

I've met others like him.

In earlier, more naive and hopeful years, they gave their hearts to a bride: a vision, a church, a new church plant, a denomination. They began with the simplistic jubilation that is found when everything is as yet unspoiled. They sacrificed, they risked, they opened their lives and their hearts and they worked so very hard. The dream was unsullied.

And then they smelled the whiff of that rubbish dump: the scent of humans. The heroes that they had created turned out to have feet of clay; the heady dreams that they'd pursued didn't come to pass. And they stomped out in fury, vowing never to be a part of one of those parties again. Now they roam alone, idle except for the occasional pot-shots that they take at others who still hope and dream.

They rage, at no one and at nothing in particular.

-　　-　　-　　-　　-

Strangely, according to the narrator, God was still at work in the mess. The same Spirit that rushed upon Samson to kill a lion rushed upon him again. We already know that God was seeking an occasion to stir sleeping Israel, to nudge them to rise up against their Philistine oppressors. This slaughter by Samson could have launched that campaign.

In the chaos and the rage and the madness and the foolishness of it all, God was hovering, moving, stirring, hoping.

But Samson still ended the day brideless. And friendless.

Book Three

THE INCREDIBLE HULK

When the Philistines asked, 'Who did this?' they were told, 'Samson, the Timnite's son-in-law, because his wife was given to his friend.'

Later on, at the time of wheat harvest, Samson took a young goat and went to visit his wife. He said, 'I'm going to my wife's room.' But her father would not let him go in.

So the Philistines went up and burned her and her father to death. Samson said to them, 'Since you've acted like this, I won't stop until I get my revenge on you.' He attacked them viciously and slaughtered many of them. Then he went down and stayed in a cave in the rock of Etam.

'I was so sure you thoroughly hated her,' he said, 'that I gave her to your friend. Isn't her younger sister more attractive? Take her instead.'

Samson said to them, 'This time I have a right to get even with the Philistines; I will really harm them.' So he went out and caught three hundred foxes and tied them tail to tail in pairs. He then fastened a torch to every pair of tails, lit the torches and let the foxes loose in the standing corn of the Philistines. He burned up the shocks and standing corn, together with the vineyards and olive groves.

The Philistines went up and camped in Judah, spreading out near Lehi. The men of Judah asked, 'Why have you come to fight us?'

'We have come to take Samson prisoner,' they answered, 'to do to him as he did to us.'

Then three thousand men from Judah went down to the cave in the rock of Etam and said to Samson, 'Don't you realise that the Philistines are rulers over us? What have you done to us?'

He answered, 'I merely did to them what they did to me.'

They said to him, 'We've come to tie you up and hand you over to the Philistines.'

Samson said, 'Swear to me that you won't kill me yourselves.'

'Agreed,' they answered. 'We will only tie you up and hand you over to them. We will not kill you.' So they bound him with two new ropes and led him up from the rock. As he approached Lehi, the Philistines came toward him shouting. The Spirit of the LORD came upon him in power. The ropes on his arms became like charred flax, and the bindings dropped from his hands. Finding a fresh jaw-bone of a donkey, he grabbed it and struck down a thousand men.

Then Samson said,

'With a donkey's jaw-bone

I have made donkeys of them.

With a donkey's jaw-bone

I have killed a thousand men.'

When he finished speaking, he threw away the jaw-bone; and the place was called Ramath Lehi.

Because he was very thirsty, he cried out to the LORD, 'You have given your servant this great victory. Must I now die of thirst and fall into the hands of the uncircumcised?' Then God opened up the hollow place in Lehi, and water came out of it. When Samson drank, his strength returned and he revived. So the spring was called En Hakkore, and it is still there in Lehi.[1]

Eleven:
LIFE IS NOT FOR THE TAKING

'We make a living by what we get, but we make a life by what we give.' – Winston Churchill[1]

It was (perhaps with the exception of *The Jeremy Kyle Show*) the worst programme in the history of daytime television.

And that means it was *really* bad.

In the dire daytime line-up of programming about buy-to-lets, elderly cleaning ladies profiling filthy houses and the ongoing hunt for surprised inheritors came a show that was truly awful: *Supermarket Sweep*. A grotesque celebration of grabbing, it involved two teams and a frantic dash through a supermarket, as contestants breathlessly rushed to load their trolleys high with the most expensive things they could grab.

The team with the highest total won the dubious right to return to the show and play in the next round of the game: both teams kept the groceries they picked up.

Rush and grab. The most successful takers win.

Some of us live our lives like that.

We sprint through life, endlessly taking.

We grab at stuff and uncaringly hijack other people's time, insisting that our needs take first priority. We become takers in our conversations, as we dominate them, and in our marriages, as we begin by saying 'I do' and then insist that our partners do most of the doing from then on. We take from our friendships, when we turn those relationships into our personal support structures. We take in our workplaces, insisting on a generous day's pay for a mediocre job done. For those around us, bruised by our taking, we become those who smash and grab.

And then some of us hear about a fabulous free offer, no coupon required: grace and forgiveness through Jesus, too good a deal to miss. We grab salvation too and then become grabbing, taking, give-me-or-else, it's-my-way-or-the-highway members of churches – which we mistakenly believe were founded exclusively to meet our needs and make us spiritually fattened people. Never mind that the Church is designed for God's purposes, not our preferences. As far as we're concerned, it exists for us to be fed, watered, comforted and encouraged.

And when the Church doesn't deliver as we'd like (which it won't), then we become disgruntled, bent-out-of-shape people – and our worship turns to whinging.

Takers.

Endless taking creates havoc. And it's not very grown up.

Some people never graduate from the crib. Or so it seems.

Being a baby looks wonderful, if you're born into a stable, healthy family that enjoys the basic necessities of life. Babies are little kings and queens.

Want food? Go ahead. Scream. It's expected. Your mother has usually got built-in apparatus to service your hunger and thirst, any time, day or night.

Feel a little lonely? Holler and then whimper contentedly when you're picked up and hugged. People will call that cute. You'll get what you want: just put up with some cooing.

Need a bowel movement? No effort required on your part. Go ahead. Someone will clean up your mess shortly and even apply soothing cream to your rear end.

Babies are beautiful bundles of need and insistence.

Unfortunately, there are some who seem to think that being infantile is the way to do life. From the crib to the grave they yell, pout, demand, insist and sob. Refuse to pander to their whims and they'll swiftly move into meltdown. As far as they are concerned, life is about taking and when they don't get exactly what they want, a tantrum will soon follow.

Samson, sadly, was a taker. Called to give his life solely to God, he spent much of his time trying to grab armfuls of everything for himself.

Consider the way he approached marriage, which is designed to be more about giving than receiving. And that's not a sentimental, greeting-card notion: consider Paul's words: 'Husbands, love your wives, just as Christ loved the church and gave himself up for her.'[2]

But Samson approached marriage not to give, but to get. Once again, we do need to remind ourselves that Samson was not an Old Testament Christian, and so didn't have the benefit of reading a letter penned by St Paul. He viewed marriage through the lens of his culture. But he was insistent, demanding, in a way that was unusual.

Remember the conversation that he had with his parents?

> 'I have seen a Philistine woman in Timnah; now
> get her for me as my wife.' His father and mother

replied, 'Isn't there an acceptable woman among your relatives or among all our people? Must you go to the uncircumcised Philistines to get a wife?'[3]

The Hebrew word translated *get* means *to take*, or *seize. Grab her for me.* As we've seen, his parents bristled at his wanting a Philistine woman.

Marry one of your own, son.

But grabbers don't take no for an answer. Even though it was unusual in Hebrew culture for a young man to defy his parents, Samson was unusually insistent in his grabbing.

Grabbers usually are unusually insistent.

'But Samson said to his father, "Get her for me. She's the right one for me."'

In the Hebrew, the word order is like this: *her get.*

The emphasis is on *her.*

She's the one that I want. No ifs or buts. No one else will do.

Get her.

Get her for me.

Grabbers. They'll milk your time. Insist on their way. Sap your energy. Suck the joy out of your best moments. Demand that their preferences be respected and bristle when they're not.

And Christians can be especially gifted at this, because we carry a secret weapon that can sanctify our childish selfishness and make it look pious: the notion that our way is God's way.

Some months after trashing his wedding day, Samson was still thinking about getting rather than giving, even though he had acted like a complete buffoon during the nuptial celebrations.

—   ·   —   —   —   —

It's hardly a recipe for a romantic evening.

Throw a lavish, seven-day wedding reception and ruin it with a huge argument.

Storm out just before the wedding night, which took place on the seventh day of those lengthy feasts.

Make a speech in which you call your bride a cow and then suggest that she has slept with your best man (or possibly, in this case, best *men* – all thirty of them).

Punctuate the wedding celebrations with a killing spree and show up with clothing stolen from the corpses.

Then head home to your parents in a huff.

Show up at your bride's home sometime later – probably a number of months – with a goat as a gift, hoping for a beautiful evening of conjugal bliss.

Get it into your head that the small gift will atone for your terrible behaviour: a goat was the cultural equivalent of a box of chocolates. Unfortunately goats were also used to pay prostitutes for their services.[4]

Make the visit all about sex, not love. The narrator lets us in on what Samson was thinking and it wasn't pretty. The phrase he uses here, *I will go in*, is loaded with sexual overtones.

In summary, Samson's visit was all about
taking what he saw as rightfully his.

After all, he was legally married, wasn't he?

The dowry had been paid. The feast had been celebrated,
even though it came to an abrupt ending, to say the least.
Now he could take what was rightly his. Couldn't he?

You would never want to ask Samson to be a marriage
counsellor. In his grabbing, he had forgotten that actions
have consequences. He acted as if he hated his wife and
so her father 'gave her' to someone else – one of those
thirty men who attended him at their wedding, in fact
(perhaps she had been 'ploughing' with him after all).

But grabbers are men and women who behave badly,
as did Samson, but are oblivious to how their behaviour
affects others. Grabbing is blinding. Samson saw what
he wanted, but didn't see what he was becoming.

They complain that no one reaches out to them in
friendship, unaware that their odious behaviour
makes them unattractive and therefore alone.

In church, they rant over worship music that is not
to their taste, apparently not noticing the cacophony
of criticism that spills from their lips, a true din.

Grabbers are blind to the devastating trail that they leave behind, unaware that others wince when they walk by.

And in a culture that insists that everyone
has 'rights', they can have a heyday.

THERE ARE NO STRONG PEOPLE

—   —   —   —   —

The world is being ruined by people who have the right to do it.

We're a 'rights' culture.

We're gifted at demanding what we believe to be rightfully ours. Heaven help anyone who stands in our way.

A Christian preacher insists that he has 'the right' to burn a copy of the Koran. Technically, he does. But, even as the pages go up in smoke, lives are snuffed out in angry reprisals.

Smooth-talking lawyers tell us that, if we've tripped, someone is to blame for our calamity. Sue now. And obviously it's important to ensure that safety standards are upheld so, when they are not, those responsible should be held to account. But have we become a sue-happy crowd?

Have we become a foot-stomping, insistent people who fold our arms and yell, 'Here I stand, I can do no other', over trivialities?

Samson *was* married. His family would have paid a dowry. He had rights. But he was seemingly oblivious to the possibility that he might have behaved badly and damaged his marriage irreparably. The bride's father was wrong. The dowry had been paid and so legally his daughter was Samson's wife. Eager to cash in on a double dowry, the woman had been given to one of Samson's 'friends'. But, in the father's defence, Samson had hardly treated his bride with respect. The language that her father employs 'I was sure you thoroughly hated her' was used in the context of divorce. But Samson was under the impression that his bride was just waiting for him to eventually turn up and, when he did, she'd pet the goat and welcome him with open arms.

I've seen things like this today too. A partner betrays or there is physical violence in a marriage. But when this happens among

Christians, sometimes the unfaithful or abusive party says, 'Just forgive me. Let's move on. You have to - you're a Christian.' Instead of realising that there are consequences to their actions, they make demands and insist that nothing has changed.

We reap what we sow. If we've damaged a marriage or a friendship, let's not just assume that everything will automatically be the same.

We only really get a life when we've realised that life is not about getting.

Samson was dominated by what he saw, but sometimes failed to see the obvious.

He had ruined a marriage, but then was foolish enough to demand what he still thought was his by right.

And even when we are in the right to claim our rights, let's pause. G.K. Chesterton said it well, 'To have a right to do a thing is not at all the same as to be right in doing it'.[5]

We follow the One who had the rights to the throne of heaven. And He laid it all aside, not to give us the right to access God, but to make us right before God so we can access Him and know Him forever.

-     -   -   -   -

Apparently it's the most requested song at funerals.

No, it's not 'Jerusalem', or 'Amazing Grace'.

In the top ten are 'I've Had the Time of My Life' and then, bizarrely, 'Every Breath You Take' by The Police, which is strange, considering that, for the person whose funeral it is, breathing has ceased. 'Highway to Hell', by AC/DC, 'Another One Bites the Dust' from Queen and 'Angels' by Robbie Williams are up there too.

But the Number One in many countries
is still 'My Way' by Frank Sinatra.

My way. A poor song for dying.

A poor mantra for living.

I want it my way. I want my rights. Give me.

That was Samson's song, too.

Twelve:
ANGER IS HIGHLY INFLAMMABLE

'Superhot anger spills into chronic
depression, self sabotage, broken
relationships or inexplicable anger towards
others that blows scorching steam at the
slightest provocation.' - June Hunt[1]

In America, they're called bumper stickers. For reasons that aren't clear, some drivers like to festoon their cars with sayings that are outrageous, witty, sick, amusing and sometimes pseudo-religious. I'm not a sticker user myself (although I did sport a large fish sign on the back of my car decades ago), but I enjoy reading the mostly mad musings while I'm driving.

Some bring a slight smile:

If you can read this, I've lost my trailer.

I brake suddenly for tail gaiters.

Are you following Jesus this close?

Others provide helpful information for the apocalypse:

In the event of the rapture, this car will be driverless.

While others poke gentle fun at the apocalyptically obsessed:

In the event of the rapture, can I have your car?

Others are smilingly menacing:

I'm out of oestrogen and I have a gun.

But my least favourite is actually a well-known saying:

Don't get mad, get even.

Unfortunately, some of us live on the edge of angry madness much of the time. We are hungry to get even. And sometimes the ultimate victim of our rage, ironically, is us.

-     -   -   -   -

Take Mark, 39 years old, an experienced supermarket worker with fifteen years' service to his name.

Just a regular guy doing his job and looking out for his colleagues, Mark was brutally attacked by a shopper who left him scarred emotionally and physically with his knee snapped in two places.

Impatient at the checkout, a man began harassing Mark's colleague. Mark stepped in.

'The shop was full of pensioners and young families. I asked the man to leave politely, but he just punched me in the face,' Mark said.

'I fell to the floor and the kicks were raining in. I feared for my life,' he added.

The assailant was later arrested but released without charge. And what of Mark?

'The attack turned me into a virtual recluse,' he said. *I find it difficult to leave my house and I can't work.'*

Sounds horrendous? Surely this kind of thing doesn't happen in the UK? Yet, the truth is that Mark is just one of thousands

at risk in the retail industry. So, is anger like this restricted
to the shopping centres and markets of Great Britain?

Unfortunately not.

Ask PC Chris Horner, Thames Valley
Police, about one of his cases.

According to local news reports at the time, in the
locality of Milton Keynes, a 46-year-old woman was
beaten up and dumped at the side of the road.

Just a few minutes earlier this same woman had
been driving in her black Vauxhall Tigra along the
busy V6. At a roundabout, a blue Rover suddenly cut
in front of her, causing her to sound her horn.

The woman carried on driving but, at a junction,
the blue Rover forced her to stop.

Two women got out of the Rover and one pulled the 46-year-
old woman of the Tigra out from her car, punching her in the
face. The other then hauled the victim to the floor by her hair
and kicked her in the legs, before leaving her at the side of the
road and promptly exiting the scene with her companion.

The victim sustained bruising to her face and a
cut to her wrist. One might wonder at the extent
of the mental trauma she also suffered.[2]

-      -   -   -   -

With cases like these, I'm not proud to be part of a nation where
anger is so rife and we have to face the truth: technological
developments haven't made us more peaceful, calmer people.
We're an angry lot. Driving can be a combative sport. Britain's
streets are danger zones on Saturday nights, as alcohol-
fuelled anger creates ugly physical and verbal skirmishes.

Children's sporting events, which should be fun family occasions of connection and support, turn dangerous because of yelling, cursing parents, who scream at their children, other people's children, other parents and, of course, the referee – oh, and the volunteer coach.

Anger is ruinous and can shatter our best days.

And it's getting worse.

According to the British Association of Anger Management (BAAM), which operates clinics throughout the UK, there has been a huge number of bookings in recent months with website hits also increasing. 'This could mean more people are seeking help, but we know that domestic violence is increasing: eight women on average are killed a month. Workplace stress is also rising and where there's stress, there's anger,' commented director of BAAM, Mike Fisher.

It would seem that anger is an issue that has preyed on most of our minds at some point. A 2009 survey from the Mental Health Foundation found that 28 per cent of adults felt concerned about how angry they felt at times and 32 per cent had a friend or relative they considered to have 'problems dealing with anger'.

Unfortunately, BAAM was not around when Samson was alive. And he certainly had problems dealing with anger. To say the least.

-      -   -   -   -

Look at him.

He is exhausted, panting for breath in the evening
heat, sweat soaking his hair and beard. It's been
a tiresome day. He's been fox hunting.

Forgot any notion of a toff in a red jacket
blowing a hunting horn.

We're talking Samson and he didn't just go after one fugitive fox.

Make that 300.

Think of the effort involved in catching no fewer than
300 scurrying, darting foxes. Hours of dashing here and
there, pounding through dusty brushland, eyes peeled,
hands and knees grazed as you throw yourself headlong
and stretch out to grab yet another furtive tail.

Times 300.

But it doesn't stop there.
Now it's time to tie them together. Your cunning
plan is to produce a chaotic this-way-and-
that weapon of fiery mass destruction.

Grab another pair. They squirm and yelp and writhe
and bite and claw and, as you struggle to tie their tails
together, they furiously wriggle and nip at your fingers ...

And now the really cruel and difficult part. You're going to
lash a lit torch between them, driving them crazy, frantic to
escape each other and escape the flame. They zigzag this
way and that, into the fields on their suicide missions ...

Pluck another pair out of a crude sack and start again.

It's exhausting work.

And so is anger. It furrows your brow and fills your imagination, as you seethe and dream about vengeance.

It sours the taste in your mouth, as you chew over what you'd like to say, what you wish you'd said, what you'd like to do ...

Look at the fields. The grain harvest of Timnah burns brightly now, condemning that community to a desperate year, unwitting victims of those eight-legged fireballs.

Anger is an arsonist. Small situations build, like a forest fire fanned by a strong westerly wind. Before long, it's completely out of control.

Samson is mad and wants to get even. But there's nothing even or just about what happens and who gets hurt. Anger is not a laser beam, targeting only the guilty in direct proportion to their crime. Anger is an inferno, sweeping quickly through the lives of the innocent and destroying them.

For Samson's bride, that came literally. Her townspeople, incensed by Samson's behaviour, stopped by and burned her and her family to death. The fire spread.

Samson hears of it and goes on another rampage of slaughter, again insisting that he wants to get even. Again, there's nothing even about it.

Next level. The Philistines come after Samson, insisting that they merely want to do to him what he did to them.

Israel asks Samson: 'What are you thinking?' and he blasts back the rationale that the Philistines had mumbled: 'I merely did to them what they did to me.'

We're back in the playpen again.

He started it. It's his fault. I hit him because
he hit me. He hit me first.

Everyone is wrong in this story. The Philistines are wrong, as they pursue Samson and they rationalise their actions by protesting that they've only come to do to him what he has done to their countrymen. And Samson uses exactly the same language to defend his next vicious onslaught: 'I merely did to them what they did to me.' Everyone is playing the blame game. And even the Israelites themselves, as they betray Samson and hand him over to a certain death (the Philistines made it perfectly clear what his fate would be), rationalised by saying that the Philistines were their rulers. They implied that they had no choice but to follow the poisonous pathway of betrayal.

-     -   -   -   -

This is the part that I didn't want to write.

Today, in writing about anger, I have been so angry I could scream. At one point, I was waiting for just one more irritation that could serve as an excuse for an outburst. I share it (reluctantly, because I'd like to appear better than I am), because I've learned a lesson today that's obvious, but worth mentioning. Anger often develops as a result of accumulating circumstances. By themselves, they wouldn't spark a reaction. Stacked together, they make normally docile souls (that would include me) ready to turn green and start ripping their shirts.

It happened like this.

I was due to speak at a conference last weekend and flew across the USA to do so. At the last minute, it was cancelled.

I then spoke at a church last Sunday.
The church leader was rude and inhospitable.

I flew to London. Enter jet lag into the equation.

This morning I discovered that my elderly mother, who is frail, has been poorly treated by the Social Services system. Like many older people, she has been viewed as someone who simply does not matter. She deserves better.

And what capped it off? At lunchtime today I took my family out for a meal, which was excellent but tiny. We left the restaurant having paid a hefty bill but were still hungry. I complained, received a smile and a vague apology and nothing else. I was ripped off. I hate being ripped off.

And so disappointment, mild offence, exhaustion/jet lag, frustration with inept officialdom and unscrupulous business practice all conspired together, formed a rugby scrum and shoved me into a corner of rage.

I wonder if, on a much larger scale,
accumulation fuelled Samson's anger?

His insistence that he marry a Philistine woman backfired. She whined and whittled him down and finally sold him out, not only to those who attended the wedding, but to the whole town. Then Samson felt ripped off by her unscrupulous father who took the bridal dowry and then took it again, giving another man the woman whom Samson still thought was his wife.

Cue massive explosion.

Beware accumulating irritations and frustrations.
The world doesn't need more angry people.

Thirteen:
DISAPPOINTMENT WITH 'OUR OWN' IS DEVASTATING

'We can destroy ourselves by cynicism

and disillusion, just as effectively as

by bombs.' – Lord Kenneth Clarke[1]

William Wilberforce was a heretic.

He battled for nearly fifty years on behalf of the voiceless women and men, victims of the slave trade.

Some of them were treated like cattle. Literally.

Cattle are branded with a hot iron, the seared signature of ownership.

And so were some slaves in the eighteenth century. It was both agonising and humiliating, yet some of those branded were subjected to an extra indignity: their branders were Christian missionaries.

The Society for the Propagation of the Gospel, an Anglican missionary organisation, 'owned' several hundred slaves in Barbados on the Codrington Plantation. It relied on new slaves from West Africa. Incoming slaves were branded with the word 'Society' on their chests. Whips, iron collars and straitjackets were used to control the slaves, many of whom took their own lives. By 1740 four out of every ten slaves bought by the plantation died within three years.

There were some who, incredibly, saw slave ownership as a missionary opportunity. The Spaniards saw in it an opportunity of 'converting the heathen' and the Jesuits, Dominicans and Franciscans were heavily involved in sugar cultivation, which meant slaveholding. The story is told of an old elder of a church in Newport who would invariably, the Sunday following the arrival of a slaver from the coast, thank God that 'another cargo of benighted beings had been brought to a land where they could have the benefit of a gospel dispensation'.[2] But the Society for the Propagation of the Gospel even prohibited Christian instruction to its slaves in Barbados.

Some brave souls spoke up about the scandal of slavery. Dr Beilby Porteus, Bishop of Chester (and later Bishop of London) preached the sermon at the 1783 Anniversary of the SPG at St Mary-le-Bow, Cheapside, London. He issued a prophetic call to the Church of England to end its involvement in the slave trade.

But slaveholders used biblical texts as justifications for slavery. The Bishop of Exeter was a personal slave owner. Moravian and early Baptist missionaries refused to condemn the practice of slaveholding. And Anglicans involved in slavery often poured their ill-gotten gains into church coffers. In cities such as Bristol, the church bells pealed when William Wilberforce's anti-slave trade Bills were defeated in Parliament.

Wilberforce is now rightly honoured as a great pioneer, a tenacious hero whom the Church is happy to proudly own as one of its own sons. And so it is all the more stunning that, in his own day, he was viewed with suspicion, and accused of liberalism and rejecting the authority of Scripture.[3]

Wilberforce fought against the enemy within. His own people – fellow professing followers of Christ – were among his greatest opponents. Not only did he wrestle with the Goliaths of the political establishment, but he was rebuked and rebuffed by

fellow believers. Terrified at the 'terror across the Channel' –
the possibility of a French-style revolution coming to England –
they were paranoid about any major social changes. In addition
to the massive opposition that Wilberforce battled against in
the power structures of British society, he had to struggle with
being described as one who had strayed from faithfulness to
Scripture: the usual shorthand for those who do this is heretic.

Of course, the Church needs more heretics.

A dictionary definition of a heretic is 'someone who
embraces a religious or ideological belief opposed to
orthodoxy.'[4] When the majority – orthodoxy – is wrong,
it takes a 'heretic' to stand up and stand alone.

Thus Wilberforce was considered a heretic.
At least he didn't die for his beliefs.

William Tyndale was another heretic. He believed that
everyone had the right to have access to the Scriptures in
their own language. But he was way out of line, because the
majority (and moreover, the power base) in England at the
time didn't agree. Tyndale was condemned and put to death
by the Church in 1536 for translating the Bible into English.

Other 'heretics' embraced the doctrine of justification
by faith. They were burned at the stake for embracing
this teaching in the sixteenth century.

Of course, things change, as those who speak up persist, even
though they are vilified by their own and sometimes pay the
ultimate price for their courage. The campaign that Wilberforce
and others mounted finally led to the Slavery Abolition Act of
1833, which abolished slavery in most of the British Empire. The

Slave Trade Act of 1807 technically abolished the *slave trade* in the British Empire, but not slavery itself; slavery remained legal in most of the Empire until the conclusive legislation of 1833. Wilberforce died just three days after hearing that the passage of the Act through Parliament was assured.

And only a few years after Tyndale was burned, his translation was used in the Bible that was placed in all the churches.

The General Synod of the Church of England finally formally apologised for its involvement in the slave trade.

In February 2006.

-      -   -   -   -

If it weren't so tragic, it would be laughable, like a bizarre scene out of *Monty Python's Flying Circus*.

A huge troop of men is seen marching purposefully towards Etam, in the Judean hillsides. The line of them snakes back for hundreds of yards – we guess that there are no fewer than 3,000 troops. They are tough and determined.

In your imagination, approach these men with me.

As we stroll up to them, we wonder and hope. These are men from the tribe of Judah – famous as front-line, pioneering troops who led the way in battle during the precarious period after Joshua's death.[5] Now, it seems these men of courage are on the march again, this time against the Philistines who have invaded their territory following Samson's latest massacre ...

At last.

For Israel, the long years of sleeping are over. They have heard of Samson's single-handed skirmish against the dreaded Philistines in the Timnah region and, stirred by his foolhardy but courageous attack, they've decided to rise up and begin to defend the land that had been promised to them.

Remember the angel's conversation with Samson's mother: *he will begin the deliverance of Israel*. Surely this is the dawning of a new day. The men of Judah have come to seek Samson out, to declare their allegiance to him, to ask that they be allowed to join him in an all-out holy war against their enemy.

We greet them and after the usual pleasantries, we tell them that we're delighted that, finally, they are rallying around a leader, coming together. They're not only bold and brave, but are showing maturity in their unity: Samson is not one of their tribe; they are the men of Judah, he is from Dan – a tribe not well thought of.

But now, it seems, they have put aside old prejudices to join together for the national good.

We notice that they have gone silent. Some of them look down, studying their feet, unable to hide that their eyes are hooded with shame.

At last, one of them speaks up with a cough of embarrassment, his voice trembling, apologetic, pathetically self-justifying.

Incredibly, he explains that they are not going to war against the Philistines. They have come to arrest Samson. He's a trouble-maker. A mad dreamer. He refuses to accept the way things are. He's making trouble for everyone. A lone wolf, a loose cannon. We can't allow him to carry on like this. We're going to hand him over to the Philistines, who are camping even now in our territory and are spreading out, probably taking ground even as we speak. This is the only way to avert a full-blown war.

We're stunned and ask them if they realise the extent of their own madness: this will mean terrible torture

and death for the only man who looks like a potential
national leader right now. And this is no speculation.
The Philistines have made perfectly plain their intentions
for Samson: they want to inflict disaster upon him.

The man repeats his snivelling little speech,
humiliated but determined.

And we wonder, not only at their betrayal, but at the number
of men who were required to arrest one man: that would
be 3,000. They certainly weren't taking any chances.

—   —   —   —   —

Perhaps it's one of the saddest scenes in Samson's life.
Now he is being betrayed by his own countrymen.

Once again, we wonder if he really knew that he was called
to be a leader of the nation. Scripture records that he was a
judge in Israel for twenty years, but never defines what that
meant. Most commentators believe that this refers to the one-
man skirmishes that he undertook against the Philistines.

But now he has to fight another attack, from his own.

They brand him with their words.

'Don't you realise that the Philistines are rulers over us?'
*Are you stupid? Don't you know? Are you the only one
around here who is oblivious to the political realities?*

'What have you done to us?' *It's your fault. You're
trouble. Forget that the Philistines are our enemy.
You're the reason they're attacking us. It's you.*

And so Samson makes no rousing speech to the men of Judah.
There is no call to arms, no urging them to heroism and self-

sacrifice. Instead, he hands himself over to them, allowing them to tie him with new ropes, a captive of their cowardice.

But, before he does, he asks them to promise not to kill him themselves. It was seen to be more noble to be killed by a woman from the enemy than to be struck down by your own people.

Perhaps he wants to hear them make some small, tiny promise to him.

We won't kill you.

Never mind that they will happily hand him over to the Philistines who will rack his body; for now, a little armistice, a small promise is enough.

Tell me you won't kill me.

He seems resigned to yet another betrayal. Betrayal by his own. The enemy within.

     -     -   -   -   -

Perhaps this is not just a tragic episode, but a pivotal one. This is the junction moment: from here it's all downhill for Samson. Following his escape and murder of the Philistines, we'll see that he sings a song in his own honour. He experiences another empowering of the Spirit, but then spends a night enjoying the grubby touch of a prostitute.

This episode of betrayal seems burned into his consciousness: the day when his own people tied him up with new ropes and handed him over to die. Later, when a woman called Delilah would ask him how he could be subdued, he played with her:

Tie with me new ropes.

Perhaps he wanted the chance to prove to her – and himself too – that brand-new ropes could never hold him.

Is it possible that Samson was fatally weakened by the betrayal of his own people?

Samson was betrayed by everyone he trusted:

His wife, who rushed to blurt the solution to the riddle to her Philistine friends at their wedding, choosing them over him.

His own people, rallying to arrest him and consign him to a terrible death.

The prostitute, who, as we will see, must have let the men of her town know that she was entertaining a client who had a price on his head.

And, of course, the beautiful Delilah, one of history's most famous betrayers.

Was Samson strengthened by the Spirit, but fatally weakened by disappointment and disillusionment?

Something similar can happen to us, especially when our expectations are high and our own people act with depressing predictability.

Like the church that voted unanimously on an expensive building programme but found itself in strong disagreement over the £20 purchase of used choir robes.

Or another local church where the minister has been dismissed without notice for the 'crimes' of asking people to respond at the end of a sermon, having a missionary speak in the Sunday morning service and using too many illustrations during preaching.

Or the Baptist Church in the USA, where, after a distinguished one-hundred-year history, has split – over the position of a piano stool. Apparently there are four different factions in the church who couldn't agree about where the seat should be placed, so now they are holding separate services each led by a different minister. None of the clergy are speaking to each other and people are afraid that violence could break out.

Or yet another church, this one in Wales, that experienced a feud while searching for a new pastor. A local newspaper printed the details, which would almost be funny if they were not so tragic:

> Yesterday, the two opposition groups both sent ministers to the pulpit. Both spoke simultaneously, each trying to shout above the other. Both called for hymns and the congregation sang two – each side trying to drown the other. Then the groups began shouting at each other. Bibles were raised in anger. The Sunday morning service turned into bedlam. Through it all, the two preachers continued trying to out shout each other with their sermons. Eventually a deacon called a policeman. Two came in and began shouting for the congregation to be quiet. They advised the forty persons in the church to return home. The rivals filed out, still arguing. Last night one of the group called a 'let's-be-friends' meeting. It broke up in an argument.[6]

When Christians snipe at each other, when churches divide over minutiae, when fights break out over the location of the pews, we can experience a quiet, suffocating despair. The hopeful are more susceptible to crippling disillusionment. And when our hope is hijacked, our commitment to holiness can deteriorate.

Hope and holiness are partners. An ability to hope can galvanise us for the turbulent tide, an emotional storm or a deathly sickness. Hope sustained Jesus on the darkest days: for the joy set before Him, He endured the cross.

But when our own people betray us, or willingly gouge and maim those they should love and care for, when the stench of rank hypocrisy is in the air, or when the voice of the bride of Christ changes tone into a shrill rant, we begin to ask the question: what's the point?

Apparently, we think, the gospel doesn't make any difference. In moments of despair, we're tempted to wonder if the message is even true: the behaviour of those who say they follow it seems to suggest otherwise.

And then, when confidence in the truth erodes, what is tangible and immediately satisfying suddenly takes on a new allure.

\-   \-   \-   \-   \-

The men of Judah were indignant at Samson, because he was out of step with everyone else; he was rocking the boat, an awkward and dangerous embarrassment.

There are coils of new ropes still being used today. Prophets and irritants and some who seem like outright heretics upset the carefully balanced apple cart with their nagging questions: what does the Bible really mean about this, or that? They scare us with their questions, they get under our skin with their bold new propositions.

Nervous, we'd like to gag them, tie them up, stifle their influence, silence their disturbing voices.

How dare you rock our boat, troublemaker.

And then out comes our secret weapon. Not ropes. Not a gun, or a fiery death.

Labelling machines.

Liberal.

Unbiblical.

Unsound.

Heretic.

Of course, not all of these people are right – but do we want to gag them all, whether they are right or wrong?

—   —   —   —   —

Perhaps Samson felt the sting of the men of Judah's words more keenly than the cut of their ropes. Disappointment with his own might have introduced a fatal virus of hopelessness into his soul. If he had held on to vague hopes that one day Israel might rise up, the army of 3,000 sent to capture one of their own dashed that dream into a thousand pieces.

If you're a dreamer, a reformer, a radical, then you need to mingle realism in with your dreaming, lest you fall victim to the cancer of cynicism.

Don't bet what you know to be true on the good or bad behaviour of others.

Don't be surprised when Christians do sad, stupid or overtly sinful things. After all, the Bible sums up our human condition in one word: we're sheep – and sheep aren't known for their intelligence.

And if anyone should understand that we humans are fatally flawed, it's Christians. The gospel rips aside the curtain of human endeavour, the notion that we're naturally evolving into something better, and offers us the liberating knowledge that we are made in the image of God and yet we are sinners. God's treasure is in us: but it's contained in some very flawed and plain earthenware. Lowering our expectations doesn't have to be the result of a cynical heart.

Just a realistic one. So keep calm. And carry on.

Fourteen:
DON'T LIVE MONUMENTALLY

'We are all worms. But I do believe that
I am a glowworm.' – Winston Churchill[1]

It's not a snappy name for a character in a comedy production.

Miles Gloriosus.

You're right, it doesn't roll off the tongue easily.

He is a stock character in the comedy plays of Ancient Rome. A soldier with an inflated ego, he loves himself more than anything else and is completely self-deluded. He views himself as handsome and brave, but he is actually stupid, cowardly and gullible.

Perhaps there's another character whose name might seem a little more familiar.

Braggadocchio.

He's a character created by Edmund Spenser in his epic (and unfinished) poem *The Faerie Queene* written in 1590. Written to celebrate Queen Elizabeth 1 (who rewarded him with a lifelong pension, even though it is not known if she ever read it), it featured a comic knight who had absolutely no sense of honour. A horse thief, he is totally enamoured with himself.

Braggadocchio.

Change the spelling a little.

Braggadocio. Braggart. Someone who brags.

In more recent years, Cassius Clay was perhaps the most famous braggart.

Later to become Muhammad Ali, Clay was anything but hesitant about his undisputed talent in the ring. After beating Sonny Liston in 1964, he didn't hesitate to sing his own praises:

> *I knew I had him in the first round. Almighty God was with me. I want everyone to bear witness, I am the greatest! I'm the greatest thing that ever lived. I don't have a mark on my face and I upset Sonny Liston and I just turned twenty-two years old. I must be the greatest. I showed the world. I talk to God everyday. I know the real God. I shook up the world, I'm the king of the world. You must listen to me. I am the greatest! I can't be beat!*[2]

And one of the promoters who organised some of Ali's fights was also gifted at self-promotion. Don King was staggered by his own brilliance and remarked, 'I never cease to amaze my own self – and I say this humbly'.[3]

The lofty peaks of success can be thin air for humility.

And so the heights of Ramath Lehi proved for Samson.

-    -   -   -   -

It's seems that the excited screams of the Philistines, eager for the torment of captured Samson to begin, were what triggered the moment. The ropes fell easily from his wrists as that strange Spirit rushed upon him once more. Wielding an odd weapon, a donkey's jaw-bone (which technically violated that Nazirite vow once again), he moved into a gargantuan slaughter: 1,000 Philistines slain. He does what is humanly quite impossible: no fighter, no matter how muscle-bound, how finely tuned in the dreadful art of killing, could take on 1,000 men: they would be able to simply overwhelm him, engulf him as a suffocating lynch mob.

Much as it offends our sensibilities to read it, we're being told that something supernatural was happening here in the killing zone. Ugly violence, but ugly cowardice too.

Samson would have had an audience. There stood the men of Judah, who'd escorted him into the Philistine camp to hand him over. Nothing more is said of them. They didn't lift a finger to help: they weren't rallied by his terrible murderous prowess. Samson stood alone, save for God, and won. The trouble is, it appears that he quickly decided that he had stood alone and the fact that God helped him seems to slip his mind.

-       -   -   -   -

He names the battlefield Ramath Lehi – Jaw-bone Hill. Was it right for Samson to name a place in his own honour? Perhaps he was driven by a stinging sense of rejection after being betrayed by his own people, but was it appropriate for him to create a monument to himself? He was eloquent about his conquest, as he wrote a poem that was an ode to self. It's based on the similarity between the sounds of the Hebrew words *hamor* ('donkey') and *homer* ('heap').

James Moffatt renders it: 'With the jaw-bone of an ass I have piled them in a mass. With the jaw-bone of an ass I have assailed assailants.'[4]

But there's One who doesn't appear in the verse: God, the source of that power.

Deborah had sung a song of victory in God, but Samson gave the Lord no credit for rescuing him. In building a monument to himself, he lives monumentally.

I was a little worried that I'd made up a word –
monumentally. But my spell checker didn't cough and,
when I checked, I discovered that I am not a word
inventor: monumentally is the adverb of monumental.

How do we fall into that trap?

We live monumentally when our lives become an endless
mission to make a mark, to impress with our words, our
gifts, our style, our smile, our ability to entertain others.

When the whole of life becomes a stage and we go through our days performing.

When we pine when we're not noticed; when we get
bitter when our efforts aren't acknowledged.

When we're tempted to an affair to prove that we've still 'got it'.

When we take credit for what God has done
and become smug, clever, unteachable.

When we form relationships on the basis of our
being able to minister to others, but tend to feel that
others can do little for us. It all seems so gracious,
but in fact it can be pompous and self-serving.

When we offer our opinions whether they're welcomed or not.

When we vaunt our successes, but build no monuments
to mark our failures. Trust me. Samson didn't put a plaque,
'Samson was here', on the wall of the prostitute's house.

And sometimes, shockingly, pride begins to show up
in the place that we'd least expect: in our praying.

-     -   -   -   -

It makes perfect sense: pride can be subtle.

Christians aren't likely to join in with Ali's chorus and chant, 'I am the greatest'. We know too much about humanity for that. We're schooled in the truth about the Fall, about grace, about the call to be servants. No, that would be far too obvious. Our temptation is much more subtle: our pride shows up, like a virus, in our religion – in our praying.

Spirituality is highly dangerous and should be handled with care, especially when we pray a lot. The Pharisees in Jesus' time prayed, on average, for three hours daily.

And didn't they know it.

As He taught, Jesus said:

> 'Watch out for the teachers of the law. They like to walk around in flowing robes and be greeted in the market-places, and have the most important seats in the synagogues and the places of honour at banquets. They devour widows' houses and for a show make lengthy prayers. Such men will be punished most severely.'[5]

And our humility is more likely to become a casualty when our prayers are answered.

When Samson gets thirsty and finally does some urgent praying, he refers to himself as the servant of the Lord – the same title that is ascribed to Moses.[6]

He thinks that he's quite something.

And so can we. Others call us special. Gifted. Anointed. We start to believe them.

We forget our sins, forget that, whatever our successes, we are sinners. Samson's piety is nauseating, 'Because he was very thirsty, he cried out to the LORD, "You have given your servant this great victory. Must I now die of thirst and fall into the hands of the uncircumcised?"[7]

But he wasn't worried about marrying into the clan of those very same 'uncircumcised' Philistines – and would have no hesitation about trekking to the home of a Philistine prostitute.

Stunningly, God is gracious in the face of Samson's arrogance.

He always is. Samson acts like he's Moses, so God treats him like Moses, opening up a spring in the rock. Sound familiar?

> The LORD answered Moses, 'Walk on ahead of the people.
> Take with you some of the elders of Israel and take in
> your hand the staff with which you struck the Nile and
> go. I will stand there before you by the rock at Horeb.
> Strike the rock, and water will come out of it for the
> people to drink.' So Moses did this in the sight of the elders
> of Israel. And he called the place Massah and Meribah
> because the Israelites quarrelled and because they tested
> the LORD saying, 'Is the LORD among us or not?'[8]

And what does Samson do as he is treated with such grace? He names the spring after himself: *En Hakkore*, 'the spring of the caller'. It's the first time we've seen him call out to God, but the Hebrew word is specific here – it's about personal emergency. But because he's prayed, in his eyes, he's suddenly become a prayer warrior.

Samson on Jaw-bone Hill: empowered to fight back. Walking in answered prayer. Experiencing miracles. But the whole thing spoiled by the curse that is pride.

-      -   -   -   -

Standing on another hill, delivering the Sermon on the Mount, Jesus taught us how not to do religion – and included in the discourse is instruction warning about giving, prayer and fasting that has being noticed as its central motive. As Jesus paints the bizarre picture of a Pharisee blowing his own trumpet as he drops a coin into the offering, He shows us that there are some things that need to be done for an audience of One – God alone.

Live significantly.

Live momentously.

But avoid living monumentally.

Book 4
WHY
WHY
WHY
DELILAH?

Samson led Israel for twenty years in the days of the Philistines.

One day Samson went to Gaza, where he saw a prostitute. He went in to spend the night with her. The people of Gaza were told, 'Samson is here!' So they surrounded the place and lay in wait for him all night at the city gate. They made no move during the night, saying, 'At dawn we'll kill him.'

But Samson lay there only until the middle of the night. Then he got up and took hold of the doors of the city gate, together with the two posts and tore them loose, bar and all. He lifted them to his shoulders and carried them to the top of the hill that faces Hebron.

Some time later, he fell in love with a woman in the Valley of Sorek whose name was Delilah. The rulers of the Philistines went to her and said, 'See if you can lure him into showing you the secret of his great strength and how we can overpower him so that we may tie him up and subdue him. Each one of us will give you eleven hundred shekels of silver.'

So Delilah said to Samson, 'Tell me the secret of your great strength and how you can be tied up and subdued.'

Samson answered her, 'If anyone ties me with seven fresh thongs that have not been dried, I'll become as weak as any other man'.

Then the rulers of the Philistines brought her seven fresh thongs that had not been dried, and she tied him with them. With men hidden in the room, she called to him, 'Samson, the Philistines are upon you!' But he snapped the thongs as easily as a piece of string snaps when it comes close to a flame. So the secret of his strength was not discovered.

Then Delilah said to Samson, 'You have made a fool of me; you lied to me. Come now, tell me how you can be tied.'

He said, 'If anyone ties me securely with new ropes that have never been used, I'll become as weak as any other man.'

Then she said to him, 'How can you say, "I love you," when you won't confide in me? This is the third time you have made a fool of me and haven't told me the secret of your great strength.' With such nagging she prodded him day after day until he was tired to death.

So Delilah took new ropes and tied him with them. Then, with men hidden in the room, she called to him, 'Samson, the Philistines are upon you!' But he snapped the ropes off his arms as if they were threads.

Delilah then said to Samson, 'Until now, you have been making a fool of me and lying to me. Tell me how you can be tied.' He replied, 'If you weave the seven braids of my head into the fabric on the loom and tighten it with the pin, I'll become as weak as any other man.' So while he was sleeping, Delilah took the seven braids of his head, wove them into the fabric and tightened it with the pin.

Again she called to him, 'Samson, the Philistines are upon you!' He awoke from his sleep and pulled up the pin and the loom, with the fabric.

So he told her everything. 'No razor has ever been used on my head,' he said, 'because I have been a Nazirite set apart to God since birth. If my head were shaved, my strength would leave me and I would become as weak as any other man.'

When Delilah saw that he had told her everything, she sent word to the rulers of the Philistines, 'Come back once more; he has told me everything.' So the rulers of the Philistines returned with the silver in their hands. Having put him to sleep on her lap, she called a man to shave off the seven braids of his hair, and so began to subdue him. And his strength left him.

Then she called, 'Samson, the Philistines are upon you!'

He awoke from his sleep and thought, 'I'll go out as before and shake myself free.' But he did not know that the LORD had left him.

Then the Philistines seized him, gouged out his eyes and took him down to Gaza.

Binding him with bronze shackles, they set him to grinding in the prison. But the hair on his head began to grow again after it had been shaved. Now the rulers of the Philistines assembled to offer a great sacrifice to Dagon their god and to celebrate, saying, 'Our god has delivered Samson, our enemy, into our hands.'

When the people saw him, they praised their god, saying,

'Our god has delivered our enemy

into our hands,

the one who laid waste our land

and multiplied our slain.'

While they were in high spirits, they shouted, 'Bring out Samson to entertain us.' So they called Samson out of the prison, and he performed for them.

When they stood him among the pillars, Samson said to the servant who held his hand, 'Put me where I can feel the pillars that support the temple, so that I may lean against them.' Now the temple was crowded with men and women; all the rulers of the Philistines were there, and on the roof were about three thousand men and women watching Samson perform. Then Samson prayed to the LORD, 'O Sovereign LORD, remember me. O God, please strengthen me just once more, and let me with one blow get revenge on the Philistines for my two eyes.' Then Samson reached toward the two central pillars on which the temple stood. Bracing himself against them, his right hand on the one and his left hand on the other, Samson said, 'Let me die with the Philistines!' Then he pushed with all his might and down came the temple on the rulers and all the people in it. Thus he killed many more when he died than while he lived.

Then his brothers and his father's whole family went down to get him. They brought him back and buried him between Zorah and Eshtaol in the tomb of Manoah his father. He had led Israel for twenty years.[1]

Fifteen:
SATAN HAS A YEAR PLANNER

'Like a gentle leopard she is supple and
spreads her unfastened hair around
her lover's feet.' - Alfred de Vigny[1]

We'll call him Jim, for the sake of anonymity. Jim was a
faithful member of a church, a keen worshipper and a slave to
pornography. He was not a pretty sight: it was as if some of the
vile images he'd viewed had got into his soul and were seeping
out of his pores. His face was pallid, his hands clammy. But
the strangest thing about him was his eyes. They were always
wide, the gawking eyes of a compulsive ogler. He seemed to be
forever staring, as if his furtive gazing had made his eyes big.
Conversation with him was unnerving. But it was predictable.

He was very open about his porn addiction. Every week,
whatever the content of the sermon, he would shuffle
down to the front of the church and ask for prayer;
after a while, members of the prayer team would stop
asking him what his request was about. They knew.

I saw him again last year - it had been at least two decades
since we'd met. His face was much older, perhaps prematurely
worn by too many late nights spent poring over a computer
screen. His eyes, impossibly, seemed bigger, making him
look scared. I asked him how he was. Before he opened his
mouth to reply, I knew what the answer was going to be.

'You know me, Jeff', he mumbled, those wild eyes boring into my soul, pleading, yet hopeless: 'You know the way it is with me. Same old same old ...'

-     -   -   -   -

Twenty years had gone by and Samson has provided some form of leadership in Israel. Forget the notion of him being a formal judge, a begowned member of the judiciary. He's the only 'judge' who functioned during a time of enemy domination and the writer doesn't want us to be under any romantic delusions: these were the 'days of the Philistines'.

The days of the Philistines.

That little phrase sums up the situation: Samson was providing some form of leadership, perhaps just the inspiration of being a hero because of his single-handed skirmishes. He had escaped the Philistines. Perhaps the snivelling men of Judah now treated him with deference. But, ultimately, the Philistines were still in control.

Take out the chapter break again and you have a shocking statement: Samson led Israel for twenty years ... and *then* one day he went to Gaza, where he saw a prostitute. There's a little Hebrew conjunction that suggests that *then* should be added.

There he is, twenty years on, still being led by his eyes. Again, the narrator of the story refuses to spare Samson's blushes: 'he went in to spend the night with her' is a soft translation of a phrase loaded with sexual overtones. The writer wants us to know: Samson went to Gaza and penetrated a sex worker.

Twenty years.

Led by his eyes and his genitals.

Another Philistine woman. One who would betray him.

The same fault line, two decades on.

Same old same old.

-        -   -   -   -

I want to put this as bluntly as possible.

There's a plan to make us into slaves – for life.

There's a strategy to clap us in chains for the rest of our days.

Life imprisonment, without possibility of parole.

When we engage in what we so politely describe as
'besetting sin', we can fool ourselves with the notion that
this is temporary ensnarement. We're back with Samson
the moral Houdini again. He apparently wants to convince
himself that he carries a permanent 'get out of jail free'
card; that he can change and be free any time he likes.

But he's fooling himself. And so do we. Satan will track
us, stay on us, dog us until our dying day. Two decades
on, Samson thinks he is free, but he is still imprisoned
by the same destructive pattern of lifestyle.

And there's an additional component to the devilish strategy.

Satan is patient.

Like a hunter who sets his traps and then just
sits and waits, so hell is unhurried.

Writing to the church in Corinth, Paul warns them
that Satan wants to 'outwit them' and then adds,
'For we are not unaware of his schemes'.[2]

The word *schemes* has been translated in a variety of ways.

Plots. Plans and purposes. Designs.

All of which require forethought. And waiting.

But we don't have to serve life sentences: freedom is available, although it will probably require some determined choices on our part. As we make ourselves accountable to others, refusing to be silenced by our shame, and perhaps seek professional help, we can breathe the clean air of liberty again. We may have been sentenced to sameness – but it's a sentence we certainly don't have to accept.

–   –   –   –   –

Why did Samson go to Gaza, of all places? Forty-five miles from his home, deep in the heart of enemy country and a principal Philistine city, he was placing himself in mortal danger by going there.

Perhaps that's exactly how he wanted it to be: a place of risk and one as far away from his own people as he could get. A secret place, where the judge could visit a prostitute. In peace.

Isn't that what temptation offers us? A break from the boring, the predictable, even the acceptable?

Gaza is a foreign city within us, a moral change of scenery, a place of spice and adventure.

Our Gaza can be a habit that we keep very much to ourselves, our nasty little secret.

Gaza might be an attitude that we refuse to change; a fantasy that we regularly revisit.

And although Gaza for Samson involved sex for money, our Gaza doesn't have to be a triple-X-rated, red-light issue.

Gaza for us might be our workplace, where we are quite different from the person who goes to church or housegroup. There our language may be different, there we would surprise our colleagues with the news that we are Christian.

Having a Gaza can mean that we say 'business is business' and embrace an entirely different set of ethics on Mondays from the one that we publicly subscribe to on Sundays.

Gaza represents an alternative us, a deliberate, different face behind a religious mask.

But when we do day trips to Gaza, we experience a type of emotional and spiritual schizophrenia, because we lose touch with who we are. Entrenched sin divides our hearts and minds, confuses us, depresses us: it promises us life and then steals it away.

We're not sure where we belong any more: at home with God's people, or in Gaza, with the Philistines?

-        -   -   -   -

What is it that makes a man want to have intimate contact with a woman who has been penetrated by others even that very day? Did Samson decide that, with one almost-marriage behind him, he would never give his heart to anyone again?

We're never told that he loved his wife – only that she was 'right in his eyes' – perhaps a Hebrew way of saying 'she looks to be a decent sort'. Her subsequent betrayal proves that he got that terribly wrong.

This kind of sex involved taking, without giving.

Using, without hesitation.

No demanding relationship, no burden bearing, no conflict to navigate. A prostitute is a sexual fast-food window and an actor as well. Michael Bader is a San Francisco-based psychologist and psychoanalyst:

> *Having studied the dynamics of sexual arousal for almost fifteen years and having treated dozens of men who find prostitutes irresistible, I have found that for the overwhelming majority of them, the appeal lies in the fact that, after payment is made, the woman is experienced as completely devoted to the man – to his pleasure, his satisfaction, his care, his happiness. The man doesn't have to please a prostitute, doesn't have to make her happy, doesn't have to worry about her emotional needs or demands. He can give or take without the burden of reciprocity. He can be entirely selfish. He can be especially aggressive or especially passive and not only is the woman not upset, she acts aroused. He is not responsible for her in any way. She is entirely focused on him. He is the center of the world. Now, of course, these interactions are scripted. The prostitute is acting. But it doesn't matter. For men who like to go to prostitutes, the illusion of authenticity is enough.*[3]

When Samson begged the men of Judah not to kill him, he was asking them to show him a hint of concern, a concession of kindness in the midst of the betrayal: act as though you care.

When he went to a prostitute, he paid her to play the role of a lover, someone who cared, someone who desired him.

By now, he was beginning to lose his grip on what was real.

-　　-　　-　　-　　-

It must have been the unnamed prostitute that put
the word out: Samson is in town and in my bed.

The whispers reached the ears of those who saw an
opportunity to cash in on Samson's sexual addiction: by
now he was public enemy number one in the eyes of the
Philistines. And so, in the shadows, some assassins gathered.

They surrounded the place and lay in wait for
him all night at the city gate. They made no move
during the night, saying, 'At dawn we'll kill him'.

Perhaps they were unwilling to take any risks. Samson's fighting
prowess was well known: 1,000 Philistine corpses piled high on
Jaw-bone Hill ensured that. So they decided to wait until he'd
exhausted himself with the prostitute before moving in when
he was in deep post-coital sleep. See the waiting game again:

No hurry.

We'll bide our time.

We'll wait.

Perhaps the enemy will wait until our fall
will have the maximum impact.

When we're established,
at a pinnacle, feeling invincible.

Perhaps he'll wait until we're worn out, exhausted and
vulnerable. Or when we've taken that extra glass of
wine and our resistance is weakened in the blur.

Know this.

He will wait.

-       -   -   -   -

Did Samson know that they were out there, crouching in the shadows? Or did he just decide that he had no desire to wake up next to a woman whose name he barely knew and, now that the play-acting was over, he despised her? We're not told.

But he made his great escape. And he did it in style.

Once again, he's an artist of destruction, pirouetting through their snare. He doesn't even make a quiet exit, but takes a solid souvenir with him: the doors and posts of the city gate.

In his mind, he's flying high: he's graduated from ropes to gates. Nothing can hold him. A mad, laughing trickster, he dashes off into the night with the very symbol of Philistine strength on his shoulders.

He's invincible. Houdini indeed.

Lock him up, set up a trap and he'll escape with flourish and flair.

This time.

-       -   -   -   -

Harry Houdini (real name Ehrich Weiss) was history's most celebrated escapologist. Known as 'The Handcuff King', he was an international touring star. In each city, he'd issue the same challenge, requesting that the local police strip him nude and search him and then restrain him with shackles and lock him in their jails. A smash hit in the USA, he was more than a match for jails, chains, ropes, handcuffs and straitjackets. He diced with death – and two Hollywood films depicted him dying in his famous Chinese Water Torture Cell, in which he was suspended upside-down in a locked glass-and-steel cabinet full to overflowing with water. This act required that Houdini hold his breath for more than three minutes.

But that's not how he died at all. He died because of a few punches in the stomach that he didn't see coming. And it wasn't on stage, but in his dressing room.

On 22 October 1926, Houdini was performing in Montreal. A college student and school boxing star, J. Gordon Whitehead, asked Houdini if it were true that he could take any punch to the abdomen. Houdini was sitting on the couch half listening and mumbled a yes. As he stood up, Whitehead hammered three punches into his belly before Houdini was able to prepare for the blows, rupturing his appendix as a result.

The show had to go on and so that evening and the next he continued his performances and travelled by train to Detroit for a two-week engagement there. That night, he collapsed as the curtain fell after his final act. It was never to rise again on the great Houdini. He was rushed to the nearby Grace Hospital, where an operation was performed, but peritonitis had set in. He had one more operation, but again failed to respond. His last words were, 'I am weaker. I guess I have lost the fight.'

On Sunday 31 October, Halloween day, Houdini died.

He was fifty-two years old.

The man who had defied death so many times, and freed himself from every possible shackle, was struck down by three body blows.

And we know what's coming, don't we?

Something similar was about to happen to Samson.

But, in the meantime, the show went on.

Sixteen:
PEOPLE DON'T USUALLY FALL – THEY SLIDE

'And perhaps he didn't know

Of his prophet and Nazirite's test

How the simplest riddle of all

Was the breakable heart in his breast.'

– Lea Goldberg[1]

So, at last, we meet her. Cue the sound of hissing and booing, pantomime style, as the evil villainess takes to the stage.

'Your arms were quicksand. Your kiss was death. The name Delilah will be an everlasting curse on the lips of men.' – Samson to Delilah in the 1941 film.[2]

The temptress who tamed the wild man: 1,000 Philistine warriors had died trying to do the same thing. She triumphed not on the battlefield, but in the bedroom, the place of a million defeats.

Delilah is the *Cruella De Vil* of the Old Testament, who stands alongside Ahab's vile Jezebel as one of the most despised women in biblical history.

> *Delilah has become the trope for the femme fatale, the woman fatal to men – sexually irresistible, at once fascinating and frightening and ultimately deadly.*[3]

She's the first and only one of Samson's women whose name is recorded. Perhaps the narrator, in a flush of literary genius, wants us to hear some ominous music as we meet her, creating a mood of unbearable tension. There are various ways of translating the meaning of her name: some say she was a temple prostitute – that her name means 'devotee of Ishtar'.

There are other translations.

Flirtatious.

Dangling hair.

And the most popular translation: *a woman of the night, or one of the night.*

There's tragic irony: Samson, 'Shimson', the little sun, called to begin a new day for slumbering Israel. Now that sun is about to set, engulfed at last to an inky-black night, with no hope of a dawn to come.

-　　　-　　　-　　　-　　　-

Some commentators, ancient and modern, speculate that Delilah was the gorgeous, spurned younger sister of Samson's wife – technically, therefore, his sister-in-law. I say *technically* because the marriage never actually got off the ground.

If that's true, did she simmer with resentment because Samson rejected her when her father had offered her to him? Had the pain of being used like a chattel and proffered as a substitute been deepened when he refused her and so now, years later, she finally takes revenge? Or did she have a deep loathing for him because her own sister, father and other family members had perished in the vengeful fury of a Philistine fire, all because this wretched Hebrew had entered their lives?

It's also assumed that, even if she wasn't the previously spurned younger sister, she was probably a Philistine. If that's true, then once again we see that Samson never did get around to learning lessons from his failures. He's back with those alluring, treacherous foreign women again.

Alternatively, she might have been a treacherous Hebrew who sold her soul – and the life of her lover – for a huge cash payout.

What we know for certain is how Samson felt about Cruella.

Sorry. Delilah.

This was one different. We know he thought his wife was 'right for him'.

Nothing is recorded about him having any emotional feelings for the prostitute. Why would he? Samson went to her as a user, not a lover.

But we know how he felt about this winsomely treacherous Delilah.

He loved her.

At last. It's more than skin deep, as it appeared to be with his wife.

And it's not just about flesh, although Samson's sexual relationship with Delilah is described in graphic detail.

This was love, at least on his part.

And, if love was not blind, then love caused him to be blinded. Literally.

But while she effectively became his executioner, we mustn't give Delilah credit where credit isn't due,

because Samson had been sliding towards disaster
for a very long time. His greatest enemy was not the
Philistines, nor even his venomous turncoat lover.

Samson was his own worst enemy.

—   —   —   —   —

They are called The Twelve Apostles. We had travelled a
long way to see them. A series of huge miocene limestone
rock stacks, they are staggered off the coast of Southern
Australia. We were driving the Great Ocean Road and
had been eagerly awaiting our first spotting of the proud,
jutting twelve; some of the stacks are 45 metres high.

But Kay noticed that something was very wrong, as we stood
there, a gusty wind in our faces, squinting against the sun.

'There aren't twelve', she said, disappointment in
her voice. I spluttered. Of course there were twelve.
This group of rock stacks was known as The Twelve
Apostles, so there had to be, well, twelve.

She insisted. I scoffed and then counted.

There were eight.

I couldn't believe it. It turns out that there were only nine
when they were named the twelve. Up until 1922, the
limestone piles were known as The Sow and Piglets, when
they were given the more biblical and attractive new name.
But the nine were not twelve, never had been and then, in
July 2005, a 50-metre-tall stack collapsed, leaving just eight.

I couldn't believe it. I wanted my money
back, but I hadn't paid any.

The problem is erosion. The relentless advance and retreat and swirl of the tides are gradually wearing these grand old piles down. They look rock solid – literally – but eventually they will all succumb. It's happening very slowly, but surely, at a rate of about two centimetres a year.

It's happening.

No matter how solid, how impervious, how strong they appear now, they will all eventually yield to the unceasing swirl and whisper and fury of the water.

They're all coming down. Eventually.

-　　　-　　　-　　　-　　　-

It was a bumper sticker that set my mind racing.

Stupidity should be painful.

It that were true, then it would make life a little more simple, although a lot more irksome.

Imagine if the human condition included an instant wake-up call whenever we did something sinful or foolish. Perhaps we could experience the sensation of a sudden slap to the back of a head. Or a jolt of, say, 240 volts zapping us in the solar plexus.

Think a bad thought? Step out of line? Stray momentarily from the pathway of righteousness?

Zap. Adjust. Refocus. This hurts, but it's for your benefit.

Sound too much?

How about a flashing orange warning light, like those on a car instrument panel?

Sadly, no system exists, save the warning light of conscience, but that can be seared, ignored, hypersensitised and desensitised.

And because of the absence of a shrill early warning system, we can wander, slowly, into disaster.

Two centimetres a year. That's all it takes. Gradual erosion.

Most people don't fall, they slide. I don't think that any of us wake up in the morning, stretch, yawn and then decide to lash up our lives with poor choices.

Instead, a tiny thought forms. The smallest desire, furtive and fleeting at first.

The erosion has begun: another solid-rock apostle is about to bite the dust.

Delilah exhausted Samson with sex and wore him down with her words. But then, the process of erosion had been going on in Samson's life for decades. The pathway to his downfall was lengthy. People don't fall. They slide.

-     -   -   -   -

It was a £9 million deal. Delilah's loyalty cost no less than 28 pounds of silver from each of the rulers of the Philistines. If each of the rulers of the five major cities of Philistia were in on the deal (which is likely) then Delilah would have received 5,500 pieces of silver. In the time of the Judges a priest could be paid ten pieces of silver per annum (plus room and board),[4] so, based on a clergy salary today, Delilah may well have been offered the equivalent of £9 million, although this is a wild guess. Whatever the exact calculation, the feline Delilah stood to gain a huge bounty from her betrayal.

To work, then, Delilah.

Sometimes I think that those who write Bible commentaries are just a little too polite. As we are subjected to the repeated bedroom frolics of Samson and Delilah, which involved the big man being repeatedly tied up by his lover, it is obvious that they are indulging in some sexual play that involved bondage. Is it naivety or innocence that makes so many of those who comment on these scenes dismiss them as being like innocuous party games? Delilah is using sex to dominate and control Samson. It would seem that Samson liked this particular fetish.

And then it seems that she managed to exhaust Samson with bouts of boisterous sexual olympics: she 'put him to sleep on her lap' – probably exhausted after another round of love-making.

One writer laments the fall of the mighty warrior: 'The lap of Delilah proved too strong for the heart of Samson and what a thousand Philistines could not do was done by the ensnaring influence of a single woman.'[5]

Their sexual relationship was a dance of death, of subjection and rejection, or domination and submission. Some say that Delilah toyed with Samson, never fully giving herself sexually, denying him at the critical moment. Ancient rabbis, disgusted by Samson's eventual crumbling, insist that Delilah used sexual rejection to manipulate Samson by deliberately ambushing what was meant to be the moment of mutual climax: 'At the time of consummation she pulled away from under him.'[6]

And their bedroom was anything but private. Samson and Delilah were rarely alone in their love-making. Twice we read that Delilah had Philistine spies hiding 'in the most secret part of the house' (as the Hebrew text puts it) even while they were making love. If Samson hoped for alone time with the woman he had fallen in love with, he was to be disappointed. Nothing was as he had hoped. But then this is the way that it always was for Samson. Others always encroached on his life. Someone was always waiting in the wings, with calling, betrayal or new ropes.

His wife was given to another. Someone was always waiting in the wings.

As we've seen, he couldn't even head to a distant city and have a dalliance with a prostitute without creating a public furore. The rumour got out and assassins gathered. Someone was waiting in the wings.

And now, the writer wants us to know: in the shadows of their bedroom lurk others.

Waiting.

The erosion continued.

    –   –   –   –   –

The tide begins to lap at the limestone, ever so gently at first. Samson's life had been a catalogue of compromises, where he had treated his vow lightly, perhaps not ignoring it, but acting carelessly about it. Rather than living intentionally, his had been a life of moral meandering, of drifting in a half-coma of impulsive behaviour. He will end up asleep on Delilah's lap, but, in reality, he's been snoozing for years. Remember? Just like Israel.

Of course, he believed in the vow's authenticity. But when he finally reveals all to Delilah, he shows that

he's been a victim of a subtle seduction for years:
'I have been a Nazirite set apart to God since birth.'

No, Samson, that was the theory: the plan.

But believing in the idea doesn't make the idea a reality. You were *called* to be set apart, but you often lived in a way that trashed the call. But you're not alone, Samson. We people of faith often believe that what we believe is enough.

In truth, what we really believe in, we live by. All the rest is religious froth.

And so Samson believed and he did not believe.

- - - - -

Erosion continues as compromises accumulate. In telling Delilah that he could be tied with seven tendons, he violates his vow once more – these were parts of a dead animal.

A little here, a little there.

And we soon realise that he has seven braids of hair. He is giving her a clue.

Then perhaps he draws back and starts talking about being tied with new ropes and then tiptoes once again into the danger zone, this time actually talking about his seven braids of hair being woven in a particular way. In terms of giving her clues, this was the closest he came to giving his secret away – once again pointing her to the hair on his head. He seems to enjoy the game and bounces between danger and caution and then back to danger again.

One writer puts it like this:

Samson's problem with his vow is not so much that he willfully violates it; he simply does not take it seriously. Like his strength and the people around him, it is a toy to be played with, not a calling to be fulfilled.[7]

So Samson allows her to edge even closer, even spinning a yarn about his hair and the loom. It's as if he is saying, you're so hot – but so cold. Risk-taking escalates.

She ties him, three times; the last time he would have been forced to lie on the floor while she weaved his hair into a loom: bizarre. But each time he escapes with ease. As the tide swirls around us, we experience some wins. And we start to believe that we will always win. Samson escapes Delilah's first three attempts. God answers our prayers. We experience blessing. All is well. We can handle this.

But deep down, we know. Delilah even introduces the threat of the Philistines' arresting Samson as a part of the sick game: she offers him the truth in a prophetic promise:

Samson, the Philistines are upon you.

She actually tells him his fate, what she's up to. By now, surely he knew that this was no longer a game, that he was in deep trouble. But he carries on.

And so, sometimes, do we.

It's not that we don't know that our compromises are mad, bad or both – we do. We even lecture others about the foolishness of their bad decisions.

We *do* know. But we're unmoved. We head on anyway.

Perhaps we become naive. Some say that Samson continued in the terrible game because he was hoping against hope that there might be love in Delilah's heart for him.

Our faith becomes vague, more a hobby, an impersonal value system than a living relationship with the living God. Notice that the writer speaks of *strength* leaving him, whereas what is about to happen is that *God* is going to leave him. Erosion really sets in when our faith becomes distilled down to dull church-going habits, values, morals, even impersonal power experiences: Christless Christianity.

She nagged and prodded him day after day.

And that was another one of her secret weapons.

Accusation.

\-   -   -   -   -

Delilah's ability to use sex to slay the giant is well known.

But her words were a vital weapon.

Delilah the betrayer was also an accuser.

It's shocking hypocrisy, of course. She nags that he doesn't love her, even as she despises him. She insists that he tells her his secret, even while she has men secreted in her house, waiting for their moment of triumphant arrest.

She nagged him. She says, 'This is the third time.' You always. You never. She harasses him with words.

'With such nagging she prodded him day after day.' Here the Hebrew term means, 'to press hard, to oppress, harass, to drive into a corner'.

He became 'tired to death'. The word means 'to shorten', suggesting that she wore his defences down until he had no fight left in him. Eventually he gave her the information she wanted.

Sound familiar at all?

Remember a disastrous wedding reception, over twenty years earlier?

> *You hate me! You don't really love me. You've given my people a riddle, but you haven't told me the answer.*[8]

That's right. It was exactly the same accusatory, nagging tactic that eventually made Samson succumb and tell all.

Accusation, round two.

But then why change tactics?

Accusation works so very well.

\-   \-   \-   \-   \-

Jesus met a roaring lion once too, in the wilderness of temptation.

The timing of the encounter was interesting. Newly baptised, Jesus had just embarked on His public ministry. There was sunshine on His back, the warmth of affirmation that came from heaven itself, as the Father called from heaven, 'You are my Son, whom I love; with you I am well pleased'.[9] God knows that encouragement is a vital weapon in battle. 'If God is for us, who can be against us',[10] but if we're not sure that God is for us, then we're easy meat, prey for any foe.

And so, in language reminiscent of the Samson story, where the Spirit had driven him hard, Jesus is driven into the wilderness, where He initially faces, not temptation, but first the softening up tactics of *accusation*.

Take a moment to remember:

> *Jesus, full of the Holy Spirit, returned from the Jordan and was led by the Spirit in the desert, where for forty days he was tempted by the devil. He ate nothing during those days, and at the end of them he was hungry.*
>
> *The devil said to him, 'If you are the Son of God, tell this stone to become bread.'*
>
> *Jesus answered, 'It is written: "Man does not live on bread alone."' The devil led him up to a high place and showed him in an instant all the kingdoms of the world. And he said to him, 'I will give you all their authority and splendour, for it has been given to me and I can give it to anyone I want to. So if you worship me, it will all be yours.'*
>
> *Jesus answered, 'It is written: "Worship the Lord your God and serve him only."'*
>
> *The devil led him to Jerusalem and had him stand on the highest point of the temple. 'If you are the Son of God,' he said, 'throw yourself down from here. For it is written:*
>
> > *"He will command his angels concerning you*
> >
> > *to guard you carefully;*
> >
> > *they will lift you up in their hands,*
> >
> > *so that you will not strike your foot against a stone."'*
>
> *Jesus answered, 'It says: "Do not put the Lord your God to the test."'*
>
> *When the devil had finished all this tempting, he left him until an opportune time.*[11]

The epic struggle included three strategies: the
offer of stuff (bread), a short cut to glory (splendour)
and the hiss of slander (God can't be trusted).

But before each of those sneering statements comes a repeated
sentence that we must not miss: *If you are the Son of God.*

That's accusation.

Who the hell do you think you are?

Remember, the Father had armed Jesus for
this wrestling match. 'This is my Son.'

Heaven hollers: *This is who you are.*

Hell sneers: *Who do you think you are?*

Accusation always comes with temptation. Temptation is not the primary weapon of the enemy. If our identity is questioned, our confidence shaken, then we won't last long. And Samson didn't.

At last, he tells her everything ... He gives her his heart ...

Perhaps he told her because he wanted to be rid of the
vow. Just as a woman had placed this vow upon him
in the womb, so now perhaps another woman could
lift the burden of it from him. Perhaps he felt enslaved
by God and saw Delilah as a means of final escape.

But it's one of the saddest moments, not just of
the Samson story, but of the Bible. The man who

thought he was unbeatable wakes up and realises
that he is known, but not loved: on the contrary.

Not only does she know his secret, but she knows him, the way
he thinks, the way he works. So she feels no need to test him
as before: she just calls for the barber and for those who will
arrest him. She knows that he really is telling her the truth.

She is shrewd. Perceptive. And mean with it.

After putting him to sleep on her lap, she calls for someone to
shave off the seven braids of his hair, and so begins to subdue
him. *Subdue* means torture. She goes ahead of the Philistine
arresting party and takes a few potshots at Samson herself.

His locks are gone: the terms used are the same as those
that are used for shearing sheep. He is shorn of power,
of dignity, of God. But he thinks he can do as he has
done before. That God will come through again and
rescue him from this latest scrape of his own making.

But it is to no avail.

Perhaps Samson's troubles began even as a baby in the lap of a
mother who viewed him as not fully hers, but as a stranger. And
now his fate is sealed in the lap of another woman, who wooed
him, nestled him to sleep and then stole everything he had.

The romantic poet Alfred de Vigny suggests in his
La Colère de Samson that Delilah was the mother
figure for which Samson had longed all his life.

The sun had set, but with no sudden, unnatural plummet.

The sunset had been a very long time in coming.

-    -   -   -   -

Before we leave her, take one last look.

Assuming that the feudal Philistine warlords kept their end of the bargain, I wonder how Delilah lived out her days. Was she constantly haunted by her determined treachery? Hers was not a crime of passion, but a calculated assault designed to wear Samson's defences down. Did she know that she was the only woman whom he had ever really loved? And when she came to the end of her days, did she decide that she'd actually struck the worst deal of her life?

Jabotinsky's vision of Delilah and of her relations with Samson is far less sentimental than the Hollywood version. The animosity between the Hebrew leader and the gentile *femme fatale* continues till the very end, where Delilah presents their child to Samson, swearing to bring him up hating his father's people. This oath incites Samson to topple Dagon's temple. Jabotinsky paints a moving portrait of helplessness and bitterness as Delilah takes her baby to blind, broken, prisoner Samson:

> *As she spoke, she quickly unwrapped the cloth and lifted from it a little naked babe, about three or four weeks old. Wakened from its sleep it began at once to cry. She held it close to the prisoner's face and pressed its little hands against his bearded cheeks. Scarcely had she done so when the child stopped crying and leaned towards him ... and indeed, at the touch of the child's hand, his face assumed an extraordinary resemblance to the features of a little child; for some seconds he sat motionless, offering one cheek, now the other, now his nose or his closed eyes, to the baby's groping fingers. But suddenly he drew back his head and stood up, quickly throwing out his hand as though to take the infant. The woman pressed the child hastily to her breast and took several steps backward. At this he asked, speaking*

*no longer in his former mocking voice, but in that of
a man overwhelmed by a violent wave of emotion:*

'Whose child is that?'

The woman laughed and answered.

*'Guess! It will grow brave and strong like its father and
I, since my milk has turned to poison, shall teach it
to hate its father's race. And so, out of the judge and
protector will come an enemy and destroyer.'*[12]

\-   \-   \-   \-   \-

Did Delilah watch as the final sunset came for Samson in a
moment, as they gouged out his eyes? In a few terrible seconds,
his world was plunged into darkness, blinded because of
a woman who couldn't care less and it was only when he
saw the barber's scissors that he realised the awful truth.

Seventeen:
PLAYGROUNDS TURN INTO PRISONS

'O loss of sight, of thee I most complain!

Blind among enemies, O worse than chains,

Dungeon, or beggary, or decrepit age!' – Milton[1]

Rhys Ifans is a genius actor.

Famous for his movie-stealing character in *Notting Hill*, he outshone and outacted Hugh Grant with his brilliant portrayal of the neanderthal flatmate Spike. All greasy hair and stained underpants, Spike exemplified stupidity to the point of hilarity. He borrowed Grant's Scuba outfit (complete with goggles) because he thought it looked cool and, besides, he didn't have any clean clothes of his own. One got the impression he hadn't had any clean clothes for years.

In real life Ifans seems like a warm and likeable man, and he is about to play the leading role in Roland Emmerich's film *Anonymous*. But in an interview with *The Sunday Times*, Ifans made some comments about lifestyle choices that made me nervous for his future. Because he, like Spike, has loved partying too.

Some years ago Ifans met Keith Richards, the haggard, elderly, Rolling Stones bad boy and was impressed, saying that the experience was like meeting the Pope. 'He's a total inspiration. I kept looking at him and thinking, #@!%... if he's still alive, I'm going to keep on partying!'

Since meeting the papal figure of hard living, Ifans says he has changed, mainly because of his relationships.

> *I've moved on. I'm an older man. I'm in love and I have responsibilities. The person you're talking to is so different from the person who said that. But I'm not ashamed of it in any way, because Keith Richards is still alive and so am I!*[2]

I hope that Ifans tempers his admiration for Keith Richards. In 2010, Peter Hitchens took another view of Richards, that he is:

> *... a capering streak of living gristle who ought to be exhibited as a warning to the young of what drugs can do to you even if you're lucky enough not to choke on your own vomit. Yet, far from being embarrassed, he goes on about it as if it was all a good thing. If he can even remember 1967, does he ever, in the long dark nights, wonder if he chose the right life or did any damage? I do hope so.*[3]

Ifans reveres Richards because he has survived. Samson seemed to nurse a notion that he was indestructible, unbeatable. Ironically, Samson's experience of the Spirit may have compounded the delusion. The thought goes like this: *whatever mess I get myself into, I can get myself out of it and, not only that, God will help me out too.*

But Scripture paints a vivid portrait of a man for whom the clock ran out, although the partying continued and he was to attend yet another one. But at this Philistine party, thrown to celebrate the capture of Samson, he was no guest of honour.

On the contrary, this was all about mockery and dishonour. *He* was the entertainment and thousands gathered to laugh at him. The partying continued, but the playboy had turned to prisoner.

-    -   -   -   -

It's a powerful, gut-wrenching image.

Somewhere around 1609, Rubens painted his *Samson and Delilah*. The work was created for Nicolaas Rockox, a well-known city government official in Antwerp, Belgium, just after Rubens returned to that city after eight years in Italy. In 1980 the National Gallery in London paid a near-record sum for what they believed to be the same painting.

Controversy has raged about its authenticity ever since, with arguments going back and forth between art critics and the art establishment. There's even a website dedicated to proving that it's an expensive fake. The painting polarises opinions: it's been called Rubens' greatest masterpiece and it's been described as rubbish.

Rubens depicts a candlelit interior, a shadowy bedroom.

There's bosomy, beautiful Delilah. She looks impassive, clinical, like an assistant at a surgery, as she coolly watches Samson's locks being shorn. But there has been recent passion: her breasts remain exposed, testimony to the sexual gymnastics that she used to exhaust him. In the background stands a statue of the goddess of love, Venus, with Cupid – a hint to the cause of Samson's fate. He is draped over Delilah's lap, deep in the sound sleep that follows love-making.

For me, the most eerie aspect to the painting is the portrayal of the Philistines who have come to capture Samson; one of their number snips Samson's hair, his hands crossed, a sign of betrayal. An elderly woman provides extra light. She looks like a wizened version of Delilah and stands behind her, perhaps a hint about Delilah's future: her beauty too will wither.

But it's the sense of anticipation on the faces of
those who wait at the door that haunts me.

I study the painting and remember the
words that God spoke to Cain:

> Then the LORD said to Cain, 'Why are you
> angry? Why is your face downcast?
>
> 'If you do what is right, will you not be accepted? But
> if you do not do what is right, sin is crouching at your
> door; it desires to have you, but you must master it.'[4]

And what happens next is barbaric and cruel.

If you're a little squeamish, skip the next few paragraphs.

Those lurking Philistines finally arrested Samson and they
were taking no chances. On Jaw-bone Hill Samson had
shown no mercy to 1,000 of their countrymen and they
knew that he would do the same thing to them if only he
could. But now he has suddenly been transformed into an
impotent prisoner. Everything has changed overnight.

Overnight Samson is transformed.

There were times when he seemed out of control,
grabbing whatever he saw that took his fancy.

His moral compass was what looked right in his own eyes.

Now he is a blind man with eyes gouged out.

That would have been as painful as it sounds. High-ranking
or high-security prisoners have often been subjected to
this treatment in the East. There are a variety of methods:
scooping out the eyeballs, piercing the eye or destroying
the sight by holding a red-hot iron in front of the eyes.

And this time, he's not bound with ropes. Ironically, the Philistines are portrayed as those who learned their lessons, which Samson seemed slow to do. And they had learned the fatal lesson of Jaw-bone Hill. His wrists were pinned by fetters of brass.

When we play with things that tie us up, bindings of sinews turn to ropes, which eventually turn to brass.

Overnight a life of freedom, his life as an immoral day tripper to Gaza, changes as he is taken back there to begin a life of imprisonment. Gaza was the place where he'd dallied with the prostitute and then swept the gates and posts away. By now, those defences would have been rebuilt. As they drove him through the gates, did they sneer and remind him that he would never step outside those gates again? His playground had turned into prison.

Overnight the person who had spent his life insulting and humiliating others becomes the object of their humiliation.

Overnight a man with the highest conceivable calling, the divinely commissioned agent of deliverance for Israel, is cast down to the lowest position imaginable: grinding flour for others in prison, which is the lowest kind of slave labour.

He is tethered to a grinder.

The word 'grind' here is (as is usual in the story of Samson) loaded with sexual innuendo: the word used for grinding has long been used in the Hebrew to describe intercourse: in Job, the phrase 'may my wife grind another man's grain, and may other men sleep with her' is an example.[5] The word is still used in crude Hebrew slang and is probably what gave rise to the stories, reported in The Talmud,[6] that when he was in prison, Philistine women would visit Samson and use him for sex so that they could father children by him.

The judge has become a slave and then a stud animal.

But then the humiliation goes even deeper, becomes more lurid.

A drunken celebration meant that Samson was called upon to 'dance' for the gathered Philistines. 'While they were in high spirits, they shouted, "Bring out Samson to entertain us." So they called Samson out of the prison, and he performed for them.'[7]

It is a pitiful sight, watching Samson dance for the Philistines like a performing animal. But look closer and see something very disturbing – it may well be that this 'performance' was in fact some kind of twisted sex show. The Hebrew word *letzahek* is used here and that's a word that is used in the Old Testament to describe a sexual act. This is a word that Potiphar's wife used when she unjustly accused Joseph of rape – 'He came in here to sleep with me' – *letzahek banu*.[8] It may be that Samson was reduced to being a performer in an erotic display. Whatever that meant, he was totally humiliated. The former mighty man becomes an object of scorn as the titillated audience leers at his pathetic show.

Look again at a gyrating judge and be sobered. What is intended as a wonderful gift from God to us – our sexuality – can become twisted to shackle and ultimately humiliate us.

What we play with may well end up making a plaything of us. Gaza was Samson's playground and then his prison. We can end up blinded, enslaved – and bringing discredit to the good name of the God we represent.

-     -   -   -   -

Samson made Dagon, the false god, look good.

When the Philistines finally arrested
Samson, Dagon got the credit.

> *Now the rulers of the Philistines assembled to offer a great*
> *sacrifice to Dagon their god and to celebrate, saying, 'Our*
> *god has delivered Samson, our enemy, into our hands.'*[9]

It's a bitter irony. The Philistines are singing songs of praise.
Israel should have been singing their songs of praise to
Yahweh, but they were silent. But, instead, there's revival at
the Temple of Dagon. It's packed out and for good reason.

In their world-view, life was in the hands of the gods. A good
harvest, a victory in war – it was because the gods were
smiling. And the gods of the winners were celebrated and the
gods of the losers discredited. Dagon was seen to be Lord.

\-   \-   \-   \-   \-

Peace-loving Muslims feel the pain of being smeared because
of the behaviour of a few, when they are tagged with a
label because of the tiniest fundamentalist minority.

We Christians can be guilty of tainting our message, turning
good news into bad because of a ranting tone. Politicians
sometimes complain that Christians – and especially
evangelicals – can be the rudest letter writers. And there
are the more extreme examples: the infamous Baptist
'church' in America that picketed the funeral of Steve Jobs,
announcing with disgusting glee, 'Steve Jobs is in hell'.

But we don't have to point to extreme examples. In
too many ways, the god of this world gets the credit,
as the God of the Universe once again has His name
besmirched by the behaviour of His people.

Much of the world is not going to get around to reading the Bible, but to borrow Billy Graham's phrase, 'We are the Bibles the world is reading'.[10]

May Jesus win.

Eighteen:
THE ENDING MATTERS MORE THAN THE BEGINNING

'Only in death, will Samson prove himself to be Samson. Only in death will Samson live up to his name – little sun – for in his death, a new dawn "begins" to rise.' – Robert A. Starke[1]

The photograph is grainy, black and white and taken years before digital technology turned snapshots into antiques. It was taken in the early days of my Bible college training, in the mid-1970s. I scan those faces, desperate to remember all of their names: some still elude me. But there is a shared look in the eyes of those women and men who stood on the stone steps in Surrey years ago.

It is hope.

Some, like me, were young and had sacrificed little to be there. Others had walked away from lucrative and successful careers to train for the ministry; seasoned in life, it must have been painful for them to be around our fresh-faced, headstrong immaturity.

But we all shared a common belief: we were going to change the world. It was a hopeful beginning.

But if we all experienced a hopeful beginning, there was a hopeless end for some of our number.

I look at their faces again and wonder where
they all are now. In some cases, I know.

Two of our number committed suicide.

Others abandoned their faith. Some married their sweethearts
and then chose someone else. The majority didn't survive
ministry for more than a few months: the harsh initiation
of fledgling leadership ate them up and spat them out. I
have no criticism for those who dropped out of leadership.
I came close to quitting more than a few times myself.

It was an auspicious beginning. But for some, there was an inauspicious ending.

Samson's story is a story of beginnings and, in each
of them, the same Hebrew word is used.

The angel had said that he would *begin* to
deliver Israel from the Philistines.

In the camp of Dan, the Spirit of God *began* to stir Samson.

Delilah *begins* to torment her vanquished lover.

But now the storyteller plays with our emotions, with the
possibility of a marvellous reprise, the most incredible
comeback: Samson's hair *began* to grow again.

It's deliberately tantalising stuff; we're wondering - dare we
consider the possibility that his end will not be a disaster,
even though we know it's probably a false alleyway of hope?

Or is it?

We're now in the last few minutes of Samson's life.

Samson was always worried that he would fall into the hands of the Philistines. Perhaps he fell into the hands of another breed of Philistines: Christians.

He decides to pray and take action. He brings the house down and dies. And, as he takes his last breaths, many Christian commentators line up to jeer. He breathes his last and they offer him a clear, unequivocal thumbs down.

And then there are some scholars who celebrate him and insist that he ended with bravery and faith:

> *Samson's life, like that of a wayward politician, is a public relations nightmare ... now, some three thousand years later, Samson's worst fears have been realised: he has indeed 'fallen into the hands of the uncircumcised' – even among conservative, evangelical scholars, Samson is considered an anti-hero ... it is my belief that Samson's deliverance from the hands of the moralising, modern day Philistines must come from some other avenue ... in death, he quite literally crushes the heads of the servants of the ancient Serpent. Clearly Samson is a type of Christ. Samson's story is Christ's story.*[2]

In death, as in life, Samson sparks controversy and divides opinion.

Let's look at his final moments a little more closely.

- - - - -

He surely knew that he was a dead man walking.

However vile the sex show was, and however back-breaking the work in the mill had been, it was all just a prelude, the overture in a concert of torment. When their celebrations waned and they got bored or even sickened by his degradation, the Philistines were looking forward to fresh thrills from a final round of torture and then a welcome death that would finally end his pain. Some scholars insist that Samson would have been offered as a human sacrifice to Dagon – the ultimate shame.

Here is no irrational suicide bomber, striking at innocents. He's a desperate man who is about to be executed. He is in a place where some of the key, strategic leaders of the Philistines were gathered: the narrator tells us that their rulers were present.

Was it a spur-of-the-moment decision, or was it planned? He needed a little help. The man who had asked for no allies in life, asked for a helper now. It was a *na'ar*, a young boy who was the attendant who brought him up from the dungeon. One writer scoffs and tags Samson as pathetic, asking for the help of a little boy.

Why?

He was blind. Shackled.

Samson's critics line up to criticise his independence through life, perhaps rightly. Now that he asks for help, should we jeer, or cheer?

He prays.

One writer finds room for a small celebration: 'Samson breathed his last gasp with a prayer on his oft-kissed lips.'[3]

And, in a story of beginnings, we begin to hope as he cries out. He doesn't indict God. When he asks the Lord to remember him, this is not an accusation that God forgot him but, instead, a call for God to take note of him, to act on his behalf one last time. And the arrogance and presumption has gone: there is no terse assertion that God would act, should act, as there had been at Lehi. Samson begs, twice.

He says *please*. In the Hebrew, it is 'Please remember', 'Please strengthen' – he uses a word that stresses his humility, his dependence, his faith.

He asks for strength one last time. And he finds a clarity that he has not had before.

Adōnāi Yahweh Elohim!

'O sovereign Lord.'

This is not, as before, describing God as he did when talking to Delilah, with the vague 'Elohim', but a specific, targeted request to the true God: Yahweh.

Yes, he is still looking for vengeance. Some seize on that and insist that he was still oblivious to the real issue – the national emergency of the Philistines. But remember: they *have* gouged his eyes out, turned him into a slave and were about to torture and execute him, after making him appear in a depraved sex show. Wouldn't you be angry?

And then, Rabbi Daniel Lapin makes this observation, seeing repentance as part of Samson's prayer:

> *Recognising that death was near, Samson prayed for one more chance to attack the Philistines:*
>
> *My Lord, remember me and strengthen me just this time,*
>
> *Oh God and I will be avenged a revenge*
>
> *from the Philistines for one of my two eyes.*
>
> *(Judges 16:28)*
>
> *'For one of my two eyes?' Huh?*

*Very few English translations get it right. Most say, '... that
I may be at once avenged of the Philistines for my two
eyes.' But though I understand and sympathise with why
the translators made that change, they are plainly wrong.
The strange language in the Hebrew verse above expresses
Samson's intent. He is acknowledging the aptness of being
punished through the loss of his eyes since it is through
those eyes that he previously emphasised body over
soul and yielded to inappropriate women. Nevertheless,
he pleads that he might have gained enough merit from
enduring the Philistine torture when they put out his
eyes, to have his strength restored one more time.*

*However, his language shows that he now places his
soul above his body. Rather than using up the cosmic
credit from both lost eyes, he prays to be able to
retain credit from one eye for the world to come.*[4]

Others have not been so generous, analysing his
final prayer with forensic ferocity. They notice that
his prayer is full of himself, rather than God.

And they insist that the Philistines, in their occultic song to
Dagon, at least have a sense of togetherness, of the corporate:

'Our god has delivered Samson, our enemy, into our hands.'

For Samson, they say, it's not about *us*, it's about *me*.

Remember me.

Strengthen me.

Let me get revenge.

For my two eyes.

Let me die!

But think again.

First off, Samson is in terrible pain. And he is all alone. His people didn't stand with him when they had the chance but betrayed him. He is the lone Hebrew in the house loaded with Philistines and his prayer reflects his utter aloneness.

Others criticise Samson for praying the prayer asking for power from God now and using the term 'one last time'. This is short-term vision, carps one writer.

But Samson was a blind, shackled prisoner on death row in the heart of the enemy camp – and was very likely just minutes away from being offered as a sacrifice. His *now* prayer is entirely reasonable.

−   −   −   −   −

And so the temple tumbles and, at last, he is dead. Thousands die with him in the rubble.

What does he achieve?

A huge amount.

Samson set things up for Saul and David to come.

He was a man of the Spirit. The Hebrew phrase, 'The Spirit rushed mightily', is used in only three biblical stories – Samson's, Saul's and David's. Samson was a significant political and theological link to the kingship of Israel.

His death was a strategic attack. The reigning Philistine lords would have perished in the temple rubble, weakening the Philistines' political and military organisation. Samson's final act slowed, or halted, the Philistine ascendancy, paving the way for the victories of Samuel and Saul over the Philistines. Samson's death built the foundation for the monarchy of Israel.

And his death put the record straight about Dagon, who was thought to be a universal god, not a localised deity, although the Philistines believed that their god's power was at its greatest in the temple built for his worship. Samson's action struck at the heart of both ideas.

Now it would be known far and wide: Samson's God triumphed in the very temple of Dagon. It was a fatal blow to the heart of Dagon's mythical power. Yahweh's power is universal.

In his ending, Samson brought the house down.

\-   \-   \-   \-   \-

And so, at last, they came for him. His brothers. This must have been men of his own tribe, since most believe that he was probably an only child.[5] They buried Samson in the hill country overlooking the Valley of Sorek, the very scene of his greatest triumphs and failures. The place where he fought. The place where he succumbed to Delilah. The only time they came for him was when he was dead. This tempestuous, lonely man was at last at peace.

And so we come to the end of Samson's story. Or do we?

\-   \-   \-   \-   \-

Hold fast.

It's called the 'Hebrews hall of faith' and is littered with luminaries like Abraham, Isaac, Jacob, Joseph and Moses. But read the list of greats:

Gideon, Barak, Samson, Jephthah, David, Samuel and the prophets, who through faith conquered kingdoms, administered justice and gained what was promised; who shut the mouths of lions, quenched the fury of the flames, and escaped the edge of the sword; whose weakness was turned to strength; and who became powerful in battle and routed foreign armies ... These were all commended for their faith, yet none of them received what had been promised. God had planned something better for us so that only together with us would they be made perfect.[6]

Samson.

He's included.

Again, some scoff at the mention of his name. But as we read the list of faith luminaries in Hebrews, we realise that it was the God who works on rubbish dumps, who works in the midst of our mess, this was the God who decided to put His servant Samson's name in there. And, by grace, our names are in His book too.

Some are completely mystified that Samson could be heralded as a man of faith: 'In a story full of riddles, perhaps the greatest riddle of all is that God can accomplish anything at all through a character like Samson.'[7]

But that's the unfathomable riddle that is true of us all. Our sins might not be so garish, so obvious, as Samson's sins. Remember this grace truth: Jesus works on rubbish heaps. On the mixed bags that are us. Perhaps it is not so much that Samson is a riddle, but that God both was and is. He works out His purposes through us with a grace so epic, it's a mystery. Out of the dead carcasses of those who were dead in sin comes something sweet. Strength made perfect in weakness.

There are people with strengths.

But there are no strong people. Except One.

Endnotes

PREFACE

1. Quoted in Warren W. Wiersbe, *Be Available (Judges): Accepting the Challenge to Confront the Enemy* (Wheaton, Illinois: David C. Cook, 2nd edition 2010) p.126.
2. http://www.youtube.com/watch?v=4RaUOUwytzs
3. James Crenshaw, *Samson, A secret betrayed, a vow ignored* (Atlanta: John Knox, 1978) p.22.

BOOK ONE

1. Judges 13:1-25.

ONE

1. Louis Ginzberg, *The Legends of the Jews* (Samaru-Zaria: Abu Press, 2010).
2. http://en.thinkexist.com/search/searchquotation.asp?search=pimples+warts
3. Benjamin Balint, 'Eyeless in Israel: Biblical metaphor and the Jewish state, review of *Lion's Honey: The Myth of Samson*, by Benji Segal', *The Weekly Standard*, 30 October 2006, pp.35-36.
4. For ease on the eye, I won't footnote each of these individually. But these comments appear in the following: E. John Hamlin, *At Risk in the Promised Land, A commentary on the book of Judges* (Grand Rapids: Wm. B. Eerdmans, 1990) p.126; James Crenshaw, *Samson, A secret betrayed, a vow ignored*, op. cit.; Lillian Klien, *The Triumph of Irony in the Book of Judges* (Sheffield: Almond Press, 1989) pp.110, 118; Susan Niditch, 'Samson as Culture Hero, Trickster and Bandit: The Empowerment of the Weak', *Catholic Biblical Quarterly*, Vol. 52, 1990, p.613; *New Interpreter's Bible* (Abingdon Press) p.859; Mark Atteberry, *The Samson Syndrome* (Wheaton, Illinois: Thomas Nelson, 1993).

5. Tim Lim, 'The Book of Judges', address delivered at the Kerux Conference, Lynnwood, WA, 2001.

6. Josephus Flavius, trans. Thackery and Marcus, *Jewish Antiquities*, Vol. 317, (Harvard University Press, 1968).

7. Robert A. Starke, 'Samson, The Last Judge', an address delivered at the Summer Pastors' Institute of Northwest Theological Seminary on 19 August 2002.

8. http://www.mediate.com/articles/newberger.cfmand

9. Alexander I. Solzhenitsyn, trans. Thomas P. Whitney, *The Gulag Archipelago 1918-1956* (New York: Harper and Row, 1975).

10. Romans 7:15-25.

TWO

1. http://www.jewishencyclopedia.com/view.jsp?artid=122&letter=S#ixzz 1JSSInGnb

2. Josephus Flavius, *Jewish Antiquities*, Vol. 285, op. cit., p.129.

3. Zechariah 4:6.

4. Matthew 5-7.

5. Quoted in Harvey McArthur, *Understanding the Sermon on the Mount* (New York: Harper & Brothers, 1960).

6. Martin Dibelius.

7. John 15:5.

8. Judges 15:16.

9. John Milton, *Samson Agonistes* (London: printed by John Starkey for John Milton, 1671), lines 58-59.

10. 1 Peter 3:15.

11. http://www.theopedia.com/Mark_Driscoll#_note-3

12. http://www.thebluevinecollective.org/2011/07/12/on-mark-driscoll

THREE

1. Judges 1:19.

2. 1 Samuel 31:4.

3. There's much debate among scholars as to whether human sacrifice was practised in the Dagon cult, without too much conclusion.

4. Joshua 15:45–46; Judges 1:18; Joshua 19:3.

5. Judges 4:3-4.

6. Judges 15:11.

7. Jeff Lucas, *Walking Backwards* (Milton Keynes: Authentic Media, 2006). Used by permission.

8. 1 Samuel 17:8-11.

9. John Milton, *Samson Agonistes* (London: printed by John Starkey for John Milton, 1671).

10. http://www.transformourworld.org/en/mentoring/strongholds

11. 2 Corinthians 10:4-5.

12. E. John Hamlin, *At Risk in the Promised Land, A commentary on the book of Judges*, op. cit., p.130.

13. Deuteronomy 1:6-7.

14. Joshua 1:2.

FOUR

1. http://www.boardofwisdom.com/default.asp?topic=1005&listname=Truth

2. http://www.christianity.co.nz/ident6.htm

3. The Talmud, Derech Eretz 1:7 and Vayyikra Rabbah 9:9.

4. Rabbi Aryeh Kaplan, author of *The Living Torah: The Five Books of Moses and the Haftarot - a New Translation Based on Traditional Jewish Sources* (New York: Moznaim Publishing Corporation, 1981):
'... a generic term, usually denoting the non-legalistic teachings of the rabbis of the Talmudic era. In the centuries following the final redaction of The Talmud (around 505CE), much of this material was gathered into collections known as Midrashim.' So, 'the Midrash' is like 'the dictionary' - there are many dictionaries, each compiled by a different party at a different time. The Midrash fills in the gaps behind the oft-times sketchy, skeletal narrative of the Torah. It adds meat to its bones, telling us things we otherwise would never know.

5. David Grossman, translated from the Hebrew by Stuart Schulman, *Lion's Honey: The myth of Samson* (Canongate, USA: Authority Press, 2007) p.15.

6. ibid, p.20.

7. Vladimir Jabotinsky, *Samson the Nazarite* (1927, distributed by Sparks, 1986). The book served as the basis for Cecil B. de Mille's 1949 film *Samson and Delilah*.

8. David Grossman, *Lion's Honey*, op. cit., p.32.

9. T.C. Butler, *Word Biblical Commentary, Volume 8: Judges* (Nashville; Dallas; Mexico City; Rio de Janeiro; Beijing: Thomas Nelson, 2009).

10. S. Niditch, *Judges* (Louisville: Westminster John Knox, 2008).

11. http://news.bbc.co.uk/1/hi/health/1170519.stm

12. http://www.newscientist.com/article/dn1565-old-testament-prophet-showed-epileptic-symptoms.html

13. David Grossman, *Lion's Honey*, op. cit., p.32.

FIVE

1. *Mein Kampf* (1924), quoted in Susan Bacharach, *State of Deception: The Power of Nazi Propaganda* (Washington: US Holocaust Memorial Museum, 2009).

2. T.C. Butler, *Word Biblical Commentary*, (Nashville; Dallas; Mexico City; Rio de Janeiro; Beijing: Thomas Nelson, 2009).

3. James Crenshaw, *Samson, A secret betrayed, a vow ignored* (Atlanta: John Knox, 1978), pp.4-5.

4. Robert A. Starke, 'Samson, The Last Judge', an address delivered at the Summer Pastors' Institute of Northwest Theological Seminary on 19 August 2002.

BOOK TWO

1. Judges 13:24–14:20.

SIX

1. Madeleine L'Engle, *Walking on Water, Reflections on Faith and Art* (New York: North Point Press, 1995).
2. C.S. Lewis, quoted in Charles Colson, *The Sky is Not Falling, Living Fearlessly in These Turbulent Times* (Brentwood, Tn: Worthy Publishing, 2011). *The Abolition of Man* by C.S. Lewis © copyright C.S. Lewis Pte. Ltd. 1943, 1946, 1978.
3. 2004 *Christianity Today* column – http://www.christianitytoday.com/ct/2006/marchweb-only/110-32.0.html
4. Judges 3:10, 6:34, 11:29.
5. Genesis 41:8.
6. Daniel 2:1.
7. Psalm 77:5–9.
8. Quoted in Christoph Barth, Marie-Claire Barth, Geoffrey W. Bromeliad, *God with Us: A Theological Introduction to the Old Testament* (Grand Rapids: Eerdmans, 1991) p.193.
9. Ze'Ev (Vladimir) Jabotinsky, *Samson* (New York: Judea Publishing, 1986) p.84.
10. 'Happiness is the Lord', Iva F. Stanphill © 1968 New Spring Publishing/Imagem/Small Stone Media BV Holland (Adm by Song Solutions Daybreak, 14 Horsted Square Uckfield, East Sussex TN22 1QG, www.songsolutions.org). Used with permission.
11. http://www.psychologytoday.com/articles/200812/the-pursuit-of-happiness
12. http://pewresearch.org/pubs/301/are-we-happy-yet
13. http://www.christianitytoday.com/ct/2006/marchweb-only/110-32.0.html
14. Ruth Tucker, *Walking Away from Faith: Unraveling the Mystery of Belief & Unbelief* (Illinois: IVP, 2002).
15. Florida State University professor Darrin McMahon, author of *Happiness: A History*.

SEVEN

1. The Talmud, BT Sotah 9b.
2. The Hebrew Old Testament was divided into verses by a Jewish rabbi, Isaac Nathan Ben Kalonymus' work for the first Hebrew Bible concordance around AD 1440.
3. Proverbs 30:20.
4. Songs 4:11; 5:1.
5. David Grossman, *Lion's Honey* op. cit. p. 20.
6. The Talmud, BT Sotah 10a.
7. Robin Williams, http://thinkexist.com/quotation/god_gave_men_both_a_penis_and_a_brain-but/224435.html
8. Genesis 3:6.
9. Judges 17:6; 21:25.
10. 1 Timothy 5:1-2.

EIGHT

1. George Verwer in his introduction to R.T. Kendall's book *Out of the Comfort Zone* (London: Hodder and Stoughton, 2005).
2. Isaiah 64:6.
3. Exodus 34:10–16; Deuteronomy 7:1-6.
4. Judges 14:4.

NINE

1. http://www.quotegarden.com/be-self.html
2. Luke 22:31-32.

TEN

1. *The Four Loves* by C.S. Lewis © copyright C.S. Lewis Pte. Ltd. 1960.

BOOK THREE
1. Judges 15:1-19.

ELEVEN
1. http://www.brainyquote.com/quotes/quotes/w/winstonchu131192.html
2. Ephesians 5:25.
3. Judges 14:2-3
4. Genesis 38:15-17.
5. http://www.quotationspage.com/quote/32968.html

TWELVE
1. June Hunt, *Keeping your cool when your anger is hot* (Eugene, Oregon: Harvest House Publishers, 2009).
2. From http://news.bbc.co.uk/1/hi/business/3661227.stm and http://www.aboutmyarea.co.uk/Buckinghamshire/Milton-Keynes/MK1/News/Local-News/212058-Road-Rage-Assault-In-Milton-Keynes

THIRTEEN
1. http://www.searchquotes.com/quotation/We_can_destroy_ourselves_by_cynicism_and_disillusion,_just_as_effectively_as_by_bombs./74246
2. Quoted in Lorenzo Johnston Greene, *The Negro in Colonial New England, 1620–1776* (New York: Columbia University Press, 1942) p.62.
3. For more on this see Steve Chalke with Alan Mann, *Different Eyes: learning to live beautifully* (Grand Rapids: Zondervan, 2010).
4. *The Merriam-Webster Dictionary* (Springfield: Merriam-Webster Mass Market, revised edition 2004).
5. Judges 1:1-3.
6. http://www.sermonillustrations.com/a-z/d/disagreement.htm

FOURTEEN
1. http://coolquotescollection.com/3819/we-are-all-worms-but-i-do-believe-that-i-am-a-glowworm
2. Dave Kinder, *Sound and Fury: two powerful lives, one fateful friendship* (Glance, Illinois: Free press, 2007).
3. http://jeffsboxing.tripod.com/trivia-2.html

4. James Moffatt, *A New Translation of the Bible, Containing the Old and New Testaments* (New York: Doran, 1926. Revised edition, New York and London: Harper and Brothers, 1935. Reprinted, Grand Rapids: Kregel, 1995).

5. Mark 12:38-40.

6. Numbers 12:6-8; Deuteronomy 34:5; Joshua 1:1,13,15, 8:31.

7. Judges 15:18.

8. Exodus 17:5-7.

BOOK FOUR

1. Judges 15:20–16:31.

FIFTEEN

1. Alfred de Vigny, *La Colère de Samson* (audio download, Folkway Records, 1961).
2. 2 Corinthians 2:11.
3. http://www.alternet.org/sex/79635
Michael Bader is a psychologist and psychoanalyst in San Francisco. He is the author of *Arousal: The Secret Logic of Sexual Fantasies* and *Male Sexuality: Why Women Don't Understand It – and Men Don't Either.* He has written extensively about psychology and politics.

SIXTEEN

1. Lea Goldberg, 'Samson's Love' in *Barak-Ba-Boker* (in Hebrew, Israel: Merhavia, 1957) p.112. Goldberg was an important Hebrew modernist poet. lea Goldberg, excerpts used with permission of The Toby Press Ltd..
2. From *Samson and Delilah*, the 1941 film directed by Cecil B. de Mille.
3. Cheryl Exum, 'Plotted Shot and Painted: Cultural Representations of Biblical Women', Supplement for *Journal for the Study of the Old Testament* (Sheffield: Sheffield Academic Press, 1996) p.176.
4. Judges 17:7–12.
5. William MacDonald, *Believer's Bible Commentary* (Nashville: Thomas Nelson, 1995).
6. The Talmud, BT Sotah 9b.
7. T.C. Butler, *Word Biblical Commentary, Volume 8: Judges* (Nashville; Dallas; Mexico City; Rio de Janeiro; Beijing: Thomas Nelson, 2009).
8. Judges 14:16.
9. Luke 3:22.
10. Romans 8:31.
11. Luke 4:1–13.
12. Vladimir Jabotinsky, *Samson the Nazarite* op. cit. p. 341.

SEVENTEEN

1. John Milton, *Samson Agonistes* (London: printed by John Starkey for John Milton, 1671).

2. *The Sunday Times Magazine*, Interview with Lynn Barber, 16 October 2011, p.19–23.

3. http://hitchensblog.mailonsunday.co.uk/2010/10/a-chainsaw-massacre-where-the-cost-cutters-end-up-spending-92bn-.html

4. Genesis 4:6–7.

5. Job 31:10.

6. The Talmud, BT Sotah 10a.

7. Judges 16:25.

8. Genesis 39:14.

9. Judges 16:23.

10. http://www.goodreads.com/quotes/show/306084

EIGHTEEN

1. Robert A. Starke, 'Samson, The Last Judge', op. cit..

2. ibid.

3. T.C. Butler, *Word Biblical Commentary, Volume 8: Judges* (Nashville; Dallas; Mexico City; Rio de Janeiro; Beijing: Thomas Nelson, 2009).

4. http://www.newswithviews.com/Lapin/daniel102.htm

5. Most commentators believe that Samson had no siblings, but there are exceptions. David Grossman is one, but he says, 'there is no way of knowing whether these were actual brothers who were later born to the same parents, or other relatives, or simply members of his own tribe'. David Grossman, *Lion's Honey*, p.143.

6. Hebrews 11:32–34, 39–40.

7. T.C. Butler, *Word Biblical Commentary, Volume 8: Judges*, op. cit..

National Distributors

UK: (and countries not listed below)
CWR, Waverley Abbey House, Waverley Lane, Farnham, Surrey GU9 8EP. Tel: (01252) 784700
Outside UK (44) 1252 784700 Email: mail@cwr.org.uk

AUSTRALIA: KI Entertainment, Unit 21 317-321 Woodpark Road, Smithfield,
New South Wales 2164. Tel: 1 800 850 777 Fax: 02 9604 3699
Email: sales@kientertainment.com.au

CANADA: David C Cook Distribution Canada, PO Box 98, 55 Woodslee Avenue, Paris,
Ontario N3L 3E5. Tel: 1800 263 2664 Email: sandi.swanson@davidccook.ca

GHANA: Challenge Enterprises of Ghana, PO Box 5723, Accra.
Tel: (021) 222437/223249 Fax: (021) 226227 Email: ceg@africaonline.com.gh

HONG KONG: Cross Communications Ltd, 1/F, 562A Nathan Road, Kowloon.
Tel: 2780 1188 Fax: 2770 6229 Email: cross@crosshk.com

INDIA: Crystal Communications, 10-3-18/4/1, East Marredpalli, Secunderabad – 500026,
Andhra Pradesh. Tel/Fax: (040) 27737145 Email: crystal_edwj@rediffmail.com

KENYA: Keswick Books and Gifts Ltd, PO Box 10242-00400, Nairobi. Tel: (020) 2226047/312639
Email: sales.keswick@africaonline.co.ke

MALAYSIA: Canaanland, No. 25 Jalan PJU 1A/41B, NZX Commercial Centre, Ara Jaya,
47301 Petaling Jaya, Selangor. Tel: (03) 7885 0540/1/2 Fax: (03) 7885 0545
Email: info@canaanland.com.my

Salvation Publishing & Distribution Sdn Bhd, 23 Jalan SS 2/64, 47300 Petaling Jaya, Selangor.
Tel: (03) 78766411/78766797 Fax: (03) 78757066/78756360
Email: info@salvationbookcentre.com

NEW ZEALAND: KI Entertainment, Unit 21 317-321 Woodpark Road, Smithfield, New South Wales
2164, Australia. Tel: 0 800 850 777 Fax: +612 9604 3699 Email: sales@kientertainment.com.au

NIGERIA: FBFM, Helen Baugh House, 96 St Finbarr's College Road, Akoka, Lagos.
Tel: (01) 7747429/4700218/825775/827264 Email: fbfm_1@yahoo.com

PHILIPPINES: OMF Literature Inc, 776 Boni Avenue, Mandaluyong City.
Tel: (02) 531 2183 Fax: (02) 531 1960 Email: gloadlaon@omflit.com

SINGAPORE: Alby Commercial Enterprises Pte Ltd, 95 Kallang Avenue #04-00,
AIS Industrial Building, 339420. Tel: (65) 629 27238 Fax: (65) 629 27235
Email: marketing@alby.com.sg

SOUTH AFRICA: Struik Christian Media, 1st Floor, Wembley Square II, Solan Street, Gardens,
Cape Town 8001, South Africa Tel: +27 (0)21 460 5400 Fax: +27 (0)21 461 7662
Email: info@struikchristianmedia.co.za

SRI LANKA: Christombu Publications (Pvt) Ltd, Bartleet House, 65 Braybrooke Place, Colombo 2.
Tel: (9411) 2421073/2447665 Email: christombupublications@gmail.com

USA: David C Cook Distribution Canada, PO Box 98, 55 Woodslee Avenue, Paris, Ontario N3L 3E5,
Canada. Tel: 1800 263 2664 Email: sandi.swanson@davidccook.ca

CWR is a Registered Charity – Number 294387
CWR is a Limited Company registered in England – Registration Number 1990308

Courses and seminars

Publishing and new media

Conference facilities

Transforming lives

CWR's vision is to enable people to experience personal transformation through applying God's Word to their lives and relationships.

Our Bible-based training and resources help people around the world to:
• Grow in their walk with God
• Understand and apply Scripture to their lives
• Resource themselves and their church
• Develop pastoral care and counselling skills
• Train for leadership
• Strengthen relationships, marriage and family life and much more.

Our insightful writers provide daily Bible-reading notes and other resources for all ages, and our experienced course designers and presenters have gained an international reputation for excellence and effectiveness.

CWR's Training and Conference Centres in Surrey and East Sussex, England, provide excellent facilities in idyllic settings – ideal for both learning and spiritual refreshment.

Applying God's Word
to everyday life and relationships

CWR, Waverley Abbey House, Waverley Lane, Farnham,
Surrey GU9 8EP, UK

Telephone: **+44 (0)1252 784700**
Email: **info@cwr.org.uk**
Website: **www.cwr.org.uk**

Registered Charity No 294387
Company Registration No 1990308

There Are No Strong People DVD

Presented by Jeff Lucas

Is it possible to be hugely blessed by God – and still make a mess of your life?

A four-session DVD filmed at various locations around Israel, including Samson's birthplace. Following on from his bestselling book of the same title, Jeff takes a provocative and breathtakingly honest look at the life of Samson and explores some vital principles for living life well.

• Ideal for small groups

• Each session lasts 12-15 mins (approx)

• Group questions appear on screen after each session

EAN: 5027957001466

Available March 2013

For current prices or to order call 01252 784710 or visit **www.cwr.org.uk/lucas** or a Christian bookshop

Help new Christians develop their spiritual life

Riveting teaching from Jeff Lucas helps new believers in their Christian walk as he talks with Adrian Plass, Gram Seed, Ishmael and others on:

• Relating to God
• Getting into the Bible
• Living in Christ's community
• Ensuring spiritual growth
• Thriving in hard times
• Impacting our world.

This six-session DVD includes a personal booklet containing questions, prayers and 30 days' of notes from *Travelling Through Life Every Day for New Christians*. (One booklet recommended for each group participant.)

Suitable for use by individuals or small groups, and ideal for anyone mentoring a new Christian.

Subtitles for the hearing impaired.

EAN: 5027957001374

Life Every Day

Life Every Day is written bimonthly by Jeff Lucas, to help you apply the Bible to your everyday life.

Through laughter and tears, and his customary wit and wisdom, Jeff will help you to gain daily insight, understanding and practical application from God's Word.

Expect to be challenged, encouraged and entertained!

One-year subscriptions available in print or by daily email.
Individual issues available in print or as eBooks.

UK annual subscription: £15.95 (for 6 bimonthly issues, incl. p&p)
Individual issues: £2.95 each (plus p&p)
Also available in epub/Kindle formats £2.95 each
Email subscription: £14.25 per year

Order online at **www.cwr.org.uk/lucas**, call 01252 784710 or visit a Christian bookshop

Prices correct at time of printing

Daily encouragement from Jeff Lucas throughout the year

These inspiring and insightful daily, one-year compilations of Jeff Lucas' Bible-reading notes will challenge, encourage and, at times, amuse you as they help you to grow spiritually.

Life with Lucas – Book 1:
• Discover how to relate better to others and to God
• Explore God's will for your life
• Build your faith in preparation for life's challenges
• Find out why the Chruch matters to Jesus
• Get to know our extraordinary God better and draw closer to Him.
ISBN: 978-1-85345-440-0

Life with Lucas – Book 2 includes:
• Independence Days? – Samuel & Saul
• Friendly Fire – dealing with conflict
• Rediscovering Jesus – the Gospel of Mark
• Singing in the Rain – the week leading up to Christ's crucifixion
• Elijah: Prophet at a loss
• Seven – Those deadly sins.
ISBN: 978-1-85345-500-1

Life with Lucas – Book 3 includes:
• Jailhouse rock – Jesus in Philippians
• Peter – Peter's life and words
• Proverbs – Ancient wisdom that is bang up-to-date
• Joseph – Daydream believer and God's grace
• Close encounters – a fresh look at Jesus through 'unplanned moments'
• He never said ... Sayings that sound sensible, but often aren't.
ISBN: 978-1-85345-581-0

336-page paperbacks, 120x170mm

For current prices or to order call 01252 784710 or visit **www.cwr.org.uk/lucas** or a Christian bookshop